BILLIARDS

PROFESSIONAL BILLIARDS TOUR ASSOCIATION

P.O. Box 5599
Spring Hill, FL 34608
904-688-5837 / FAX 904-686-5515

PBTA

Commissioner:
Don Mackey

Acting President:
Jack Stenner

Vice President:
Jack Stenner

Secretary/Treasurer:
Sammy Jones

Officers:
Allen Hopkins
Matt Braun
Kim Davenport
Nick Varner
Johnny Archer

PBA

President:
Allen Hopkins

Vice President:
Paul Brienza

Secretary/Treasurer:
Sammy Jones

Officers:
Nick Varner
Mike Sigel
Jim Rempe
C.J. Wiley
Johnny Archer
Howard Vicory
Jeff Carter

Specification Committee:
Jeff Carter

BILLIARDS

OFFICIAL
RULES
&
RECORDS
BOOK

Dawn Meurin

A division of Shapolsky Publishers, Inc.

*To all the players who are dedicated
to this wonderful sport.*

Billiards: Official Rules, Records &Player Profiles

S.P.I. BOOKS
A division of Shapolsky Publishers, Inc.

ISBN 1-56171-210-8

For any additional information, contact:

S.P.I. BOOKS/Shapolsky Publishers, Inc.
136 West 22nd Street
New York, NY 10011
212/633-2022 / FAX 212/633-2123

Manufactured in the United States of America

10 9 8 7 6 5 4 3 2 1

Contents

Letter from the PBTA Commissioner

Dear Reader:

On behalf of the Professional Billiards Tour Association (PBTA), I would like to extend to you our sincere thanks for purchasing the new *Official Rules and Records Book*.

The Professional Billiards Tour was formed as the administrative body for the Men's Professional Billiards Association (the MPBA was formed in 1984) in order to develop and promote professional billiards. The PBTA is the governing body for professional pool. As far back as the 1920s, professional pool was played throughout the United States in various urban pool rooms where the "big boys" tended to gather. As the years went by, the "Tour" stayed very much alive in cities like New York, Philadelphia, Detroit, and Chicago as names like Ponzi, Greenleaf, Caras, Balsis, Lassiter, Crane, and Mosconi patrolled the country in search of a game.

Today, professional pool is bigger and better than ever. A new generation of greats has come forth and has ignited a new surge of popularity for our sport. Names like Johnny Archer, Kim Davenport, Buddy Hall, Allen Hopkins, Jim Rempe, Mike Sigel, Earl Strickland, and Nick Varner—hailing from towns and cities across America—are now joined by a host of stars from all over the world, including Nicklas Bergendorff, Mikael Hallgren, Edgar Nickel, Oliver Ortmann, Jose Parica, Efren Reyes, and Tom Storm.

In 1993, the Pro Billiards Tour will present major pro tournaments in over twenty cities across America. We invite you, along with your friends and family, to come to a Pro Billiards Tour event to see the greatest pool players on earth. For information on tour events, or other areas of concern related to pool, please call the Pro Billiards Tour office at (904) 688-5837, 9:00 A.M. to 5:00 P.M. E.S.T.

We thank you for your support of professional pool and hope that you are completely satisfied with our new rule book.

Respectfully,

Don Mackey
Commissioner

Allen Hopkins
World Pocket Billiard Champion

Letter from the MPBA President

Dear Friends,

In late 1984, a committee of professional players were appointed by their peers to meet and form a players' association. This body of players would become the Men's Professional Billiards Association (MPBA). Terry Bell was elected as the MPBA's first president. Sanctioning codes and guidelines were agreed upon. Membership criteria, dress codes, and codes of conduct were initiated. All of the things needed to make the association uniform and organized would be considered.

Over the years, the MPBA has continued to move forward, consistently retaining the membership and loyalty of virtually every major talent in the pool world. In 1991, the MPBA created the Professional Billiards Tour Association (PBTA). Unlike the MPBA, whose board consists of players only from the association, the PBTA's board is made up of players and successful businessmen, who include Don Mackey (Commissioner), Jack Stenner (Vice President), and board member Matt Braun. These three men, along with the player representatives on the PBTA board, provided a cohesive body that would be empowered to contract the necessary elements for marketing, promoting, and seeking media visibility for pool as a professional sport.

The MPBA, the home of the world's greatest professional players, proudly endorses this rulebook and believes it to be the finest and most complete book of its kind in the world.

Sincerely,

Allen Hopkins
MPBA President

The History of
American Professional Billiards

Billiards has been with us for about 500 years. It has been played for money for almost as long. The first book in English on billiards, *Cotton's Compleat Gamester*, published in 1674, contains warnings against betting with strangers. However, it was not until the 1850s that a class of fulltime professional players developed, not long after the establishment of public rooms devoted entirely to billiards. This article concentrates on professional pocket, or pool, games rather than the carom variety.

"Pool" is a term used to describe games whose object is to sink balls in pockets. The term originally referred to any type of amusement in which players put bets into a pot, or "pool." By coincidence, after the invention of the telegraph in the mid-nineteenth century, off-track betting parlors known as "pool-rooms" were opened. To provide recreation for patrons who had to wait between races, these rooms installed tables for playing pool, and the association between the game of pool and "pool-rooms" where men loitered to bet on horses unfortunately became fixed in the public mind. Professional players have suffered because of this connection ever since.

The chief American billiards game, until the 1870s, was American Four Ball billiards, usually played on a large (eleven- or twelve-foot), four- or six-pocket table with four balls—two white and two red. It was derived directly from English billiards, and points could be scored by pocketing balls, scratching the cue ball off an object ball, or by making caroms on two or three balls. By combining different scoring opportunities, it was possible to make up to 13 points on a single shot. Because more than one point could be achieved on a stroke, the final scores of Four Ball matches were usually not whole multiples of 100, but might be 1,503 to 1,221, for example.

The notion of charging admission to the public to watch other people play for money did not develop until shortly before the Civil War. On April 10, 1859, in the first billiards event with a paying audience, Dudley Kavanagh beat Michael Foley, 1000 to 989, in an exciting match for $1,000 in Detroit at Firemen's Hall, the largest public building in the city. Spectators were charged five dollars each to get in in a day when seats at the theater cost less than a quarter. At twenty times the cost of a theater ticket, the equivalent price today would be a thousand dollars!

The next evening in the same hall, Michael Phelan beat John Seereiter for the astronomical prize of $15,000. In present dollars, there has never been as large a purse in this country since then. Phelan was the father of American billiards. He wrote the first billiards book published in the United States, invented new types of cushions, added diamonds to the table, wrote a weekly column on billiards, and was a competitive player. He formed a table-manufacturing concern that later merged to form the Brunswick-Balke-Collender Company, which controlled professional play from the 1880s until the 1950s.

The first professional tournament held in the United States was at Phelan and Collender's rooms in New York in 1860. The prize was two cue sticks and first place was won by Dudley Kavanagh. It was usual at the time to add jeweled cues and a full-size table to the cash prize for first place in such events—which could amount to as much as a few thousand dollars.

Matches were very formal and lengthy. Each player was represented by a second, called an umpire, whose job was to look out for the player's interests during the match. The umpires chose the referee, who was to preside over the event and even had the power to nullify bets among the spectators if he felt the contest was not being played fairly. The tournament organizers supplied a marker, who was charged with keeping the score accurately—not an easy chore when up to 13 points could be scored on one shot and game total might be 1,500. Betting was permitted, and the crowds were boisterous, most spectators having a financial interest in the outcome.

The players did not have an easy time. Halls were poorly heated, and light came from open gas burners, which were noisy and provided uneven light. Flies might become singed in the flames and drop onto the table. The Phelan-Seereiter match lasted about eight hours and was an endurance contest for both audience and players. However, the magnitude of the prize established professional billiards as the country's premiere spectator sport, rivaling only racing in popularity.

Between 1860 and 1880, Four Ball died away completely and was replaced by two games: Straight Rail billiards, played on a pocketless table, and Fifteen Ball pool, played with fifteen object balls on a six-pocket table. All carom games derive from Straight Rail, while all American pool games are descendants of Fifteen Ball. In Fifteen Ball pool, each ball has a numerical value from 1 to 15. The opening breaker hits the full

17

rack with the object of sinking as many balls as possible. If he is successful, he keeps shooting until he misses. Each ball pocketed counts for as many points as the number on the ball, but there is no requirement to hit the balls in any particular order. Since the total of the numbers 1 through 15 is 120, a player wins a rack when he scores more than half of 120, or 61 points. For this reason, the game was sometimes known as 61 Pool. A match was usually a race to 21 racks.

The first American pool championship was decided by a ten-player round-robin tournament in New York in April 1878. The game was American Fifteen Ball pool, race to 11, won by Cyrille Dion of Canada, who took home the first prize of $250. For the next three years, the title changed hands only by challenge matches. The next title tournament was not held until 1881. It was many years before there was an annual title competition, so it is generally wrong to associate a championship with a particular year. Meanwhile, ten-foot tables became standard for pool games.

Originally, only the ball to be pocketed had to be called. Calling both ball and pocket was not required until 1884. The scoring method of Fifteen Ball pool made it possible to win a game by sinking only five balls (11 through 15). This method was felt to be unfair, and the new game of Continuous Pool appeared in title play in 1889. In this game, the same equipment was used, but each ball was worth one point and the score was kept "continuously" from one rack to the next. There was no break ball yet—on each rack, the player who sank the last ball of the previous rack had to break open a full pack. No ball had to be called on the break. Continuous Pool title matches were usually 600 points, played in blocks of 200 points per session for three consecutive nights. Even if a player reached a multiple of 200, play would not be halted in the middle of a rack, but would be allowed to continue until all object balls were pocketed. So . . . the score after two nights might be something like 407 to 364.

Over the years, the pool title has been decided in three different ways: by challenge match, tournament, and league play. The holder of the title normally had to accept a challenge from anyone if it was accompanied by a cash stake, and had to play for the title within a short period, usually 60 days. This meant he could be forced to defend six more times during a year. The amount of the required stake was large enough to discourage unskilled competitors from staging a title match simply to achieve notoriety. If the money was properly posted and the champion refused to accept the challenge, the title passed to the challenger by forfeit. The title has been lost in this manner about a dozen times, all prior to 1935.

New York has been the scene of title competition seventy-four times, the most of any city. Chicago is the runner-up with seventeen. The smallest town in which the title has been won is Sedalia, Missouri, Johnny Layton's home, in 1916.

When the title granted by a sponsor expired, the title would become vacant until a tournament could be held to crown a new champion. Tournaments were exclusively round-robin or double round-robin events until 1976, when the double-elimination format was introduced. (In a double round-robin, each player meets every other player twice.) While in recent decades the tournament format has dominated play, out of the more than two hundred times the title has changed hands since 1878, only sixty-one have been by tournament. The two-player challenge match has been the principal mode of competition. The record books have not been very careful to distinguish between national and world championships. The situation is somewhat akin to baseball: The "World" Series is really the U.S. (and now Canadian) championship. So it was in pool. There was no international sanctioning body for professional billiards, so the United States was free to call its national championship a "world" event.

Early in the twentieth century, players had become so skilled at Continuous Pool that safety play was an important consideration. If the opponent had the capability of running 60 points in a 100-point match, it was critical not to let him have the chance. Therefore, the best players became fearful of taking break shots, which could leave the pack spread without sinking anything. So they began to play safe at the beginning of each rack, and games slowed to a crawl. In 1910, Jerome Keogh of Rochester, who had been champion ten times, suggested leaving the fifteenth ball of each rack on the table, racking the other fourteen, and using the lone ball to split the rack to thus avoid the risk of an open break. The new game was called 14.1 Continuous; that is, Continuous Pool in which fourteen balls are racked and one is left free. The "point" in "Fourteen Point One" was borrowed from balkline, an old carom game with versions like "18.1" and "14.2." Within a decade or so, 14.1 Continuous became known as Straight Pool.

The new game officially replaced Continuous Pool as the championship game in 1912. In an effort to eliminate the negative connotation of the word "Pool," it was called "Pocket Billiards"—which capitalized on the idea that billiards was somehow more genteel, as if removing the pockets from the table somehow purified the game. No one had ever run 100 in a title Continuous Pool match, because of the lack of a break ball. Alfredo de Oro pushed the record to 96, where it still stands, probably because the game hasn't been played since 1911. The first player to run over 100 in a Straight Pool match was Emmett Blankenship, around 1915, with a run of 141. Frank Taberski had exactly 100 in 1921; Crane reached 309 in 1939; and Mosconi, a stratospheric 526 in 1954.

On three occasions the title has changed hands after a grueling season of league play, somewhat similar to major-league baseball. A room in each city that was involved would sponsor a player, who would travel around playing matches in other cities. The player with the best record would take the title. Willie Mosconi won his first championship in 1941 this way, with a record of 176 to 48 after 224 games of 125 points in eight cities extending over more than five months. He ran 125 and out seven times during the season, all on 5-by-10 tables.

During the 1920s, winning the world title was a lucrative proposition. The winner received a cash prize, usually several thousand dollars in an era when this was more than an average annual wage, a percentage of the gate receipts, and a full-time salary of another few thousand dollars for which his responsibilities were to travel the country promoting billiards, all expenses paid. In addition, there was the opportunity to earn money from product endorsements, lessons, and exhibition play. The number of pool rooms in the country was so large that it was even possible to stay on the road giving demonstrations continuously to large and knowledgeable audiences.

By the 1930s, it had become common for tournament players to lose 60 points in scratches during a 125-point match. The game was again becoming boring, so experiments were conducted to find ways of eliminating safety play. One was to impose a severe penalty for more than two unsuccessful safeties in a row. Another was to give the incoming player the cue ball behind the head string on the opening shot of every inning, and to require the referee to move the ball lying closest to the center string onto the center spot—in essence, guaranteeing the player a nice break-shot opportunity every inning. Eventually, the decision was made to increase the cost of three consecutive scratches, which now stands at 20 percent of game total, or 30 points in a 150-point game.

The method of choosing the players who would participate in title tournaments was highly controversial. There was no notion of a truly open tournament until the 1960s. Brunswick sponsored and controlled the events, selecting players by invitation. For a time, several slots were filled by players who won sectional tournaments around the country, but these players rarely finished anywhere but at the bottom, and eventually this method of qualifying was dropped. The tournament sponsor then wielded tremendous power and did not hesitate to exclude players who caused trouble by asking for more money or engaged in disruptive behavior. Mosconi, Greenleaf, Hoppe, and Ponzi were all involved in legal disputes with Brunswick over tournament eligibility. Nevertheless, it was to the interest of both players and sponsors to provide the best competition; and differences were resolved.

The player with the most outright pocket billiards titles was Alfredo de Oro, who won or successfully defended the crown thirty-two times during the period 1887-1913. He is the only person ever to win titles at all three forms of the game: Fifteen Ball, Continuous Pool, and Straight Pool. (He was also

simultaneously the world three-cushion champion several times.)
Greenleaf is second in titles with twenty, Mosconi third with
nineteen. Greenleaf and Taberski each won ten consecutive
times. Irving Crane has come in second thirteen times, more
than anyone else. Considering the number of different competitors, Straight Pool has really been dominated by a very small
circle of great players. Between 1917 and 1956, only eight
different people held the title even though it was on the line in
competition on sixty-nine different occasions during that time.

The size of the championship table was reduced to 4 1/2
by 9 feet in 1949, partially to reduce Irving Crane's height
advantage. At more than six feet, he towered over all other top
competitors, including Mosconi, Caras, and Andrew Ponzi.
Changing the table size may have worked. Out of the next
eleven title events, Mosconi won ten, Crane only one.

Eventually, as with other forms of billiards, the skill of
the players contributed to the demise of the game. It's not very
interesting to watch players who never seem to miss. When
Willie Mosconi retired in 1956 for health reasons, championship Straight Pool retired with him. It was revived by the Billiards Congress of America's U.S. Open competition in 1966,
but the event has recently been held only irregularly—to the
dismay of purists who consider Straight Pool to be the ultimate
competitive test.

Nine Ball and One Pocket were played in Johnston City
and Las Vegas tournaments during the 1960s, when they were
still regarded as hustler's games. Nine Ball did not become a
recognized title event until the '70s, but it quickly surpassed
Straight Pool in popularity. Since that time, tournament formats
have been heavily influenced by the requirements of television.

The trend has been to shorten the games and matches so that more action can be presented in a short time, with breaks for commercials. The most recent Nine Ball variation along these lines is Pro Express, in which all balls except the nine remain pocketed, even if sunk illegally. The game goes so fast that slow-motion replay may be required.

The skill of the current professionals is astounding, even when viewed in comparison with heroes of the past. Their accomplishments can only be recognized properly through exposure, which in turn requires a community of fans who want to watch pool, not just play it. History has shown that when a game increases in popularity, as pool has done, the public takes a greater interest in the top performers. May the PBTA derive every benefit from today's resurgence of interest in pool.

Mike Shamos,
Curator, The Billiards Archive

The Billiards Archive is a nonprofit organization that preserves the history of pool, billiards, and snooker.

Basic Instruction
by the Pros

There are many instructional books on the market for today's pocket billiards player. Although the contents of each book may vary, most all describe the basic fundamentals of playing the game.

Knowing the importance of this valuable information, the PBTA has included in its book a section on the basics.

When you are watching the top professional players, you may notice differences in their style of play. For example, one may stand with both legs straight while the other bends one knee, etc. Since everyone has his or her own method of playing and teaching, the PBTA decided to interview some of the pros on this subject. This is what they had to say.

STANCE

MIKE SIGEL

"The stance depends greatly on your height and weight. A good guideline to follow would be that your feet are well balanced and your weight is distributed evenly. It is very important to feel comfortable."

NICK VARNER

"Your feet should be spread apart wider than your shoulders. Distribute the weight evenly on both feet. Place your feet at roughly a forty-five-degree angle. Bend over from the waist with your chin and nose directly over the shaft of the cue stick. Head position varies from almost touching the shaft with your chin to maybe six inches above the shaft.''

ALLEN HOPKINS
''The stance depends a lot on the size of your body and the way you feel comfortable aiming the cue ball at the object ball. Some people get down really low on a shot, so that their chin is usually directly over the shaft of the cue. Others stay high on a shot, so they aim differently and stand differently. Always keep your balance, so that you don't feel like you are going to fall over. This will help your power and accuracy.''

JIM REMPE
''Your feet should be spread apart at least wider than your shoulders. Make sure that both legs are not in a direct line with the shot. The back foot should be directly under the stroking arm, and the other foot should be to the left of the cue stick line. The bridge hand is straight out from the back foot. This way, you will have a tripod between the bridge hand and your feet, so your pressure points will be as they should be for better balance.''

EARL STRICKLAND
''Break both knees slightly to get a good comfortable stance. Your back foot should be at 3 o'clock and your front foot at 12 to 1 o'clock.''

KIM DAVENPORT

"I like to be very firm in my stance—solid and balanced. It is not good to feel tight."

BUDDY HALL

"It really depends on the height of the person. Tall people tend to bend both knees. They have a spread-eagle stance of about 2 to 3 feet and need to bend both knees a little, where shorter people might only bend the front leg. It's whatever you can do to get the best balance. You don't want to put too much stress on your joints by locking them."

GRIP

KIM DAVENPORT

"Do not hold your cue stick in the back too tight or too loose. Hold it like you have a bird in your hand and you don't want to hurt him or let him go."

EARL STRICKLAND

"You should use all five fingers on your grip. When more draw is needed, loosen the grip slightly. When using extreme draw, use a slip stroke."

MIKE SIGEL

"Your grip should be loose and pivot on the second and third fingers. Use the other fingers as guides. As you follow through, you will grip tighter. Naturally, the hand should fall directly under the elbow when in the shooting position."

ALLEN HOPKINS

"Hold the cue stick firmly but not tight. You must guide the cue stick with the fingers that feel the most comfortable and help, to be the most accurate. When you practice your stroke, you can experiment then and see which feels best to you."

JIM REMPE

"Use the two middle fingers instead of the index finger and you will notice that on the follow through your wrist will go straighter—which means your stroke is straighter."

BUDDY HALL

"I hold the back of the cue with my whole hand. Every finger on my hand touches the cue, but I don't hold the cue tight."

BRIDGES

NICK VARNER

"The easiest bridge to make is the open-hand bridge. Spread four fingers of the hand with the heel of the hand resting on the table. Put the thumb against the index finger to form a channel between the knuckle of the index finger and the thumb. Curl the thumb so that channel is more defined. The open-hand bridge makes it easy to aim, because the loop from your index finger on a closed bridge is not in the way. On the closed bridge, the loop gives you more control on hitting the cue ball accurately and for control in playing position. It is more difficult to make the looped bridge."

JIM REMPE

"There are many different bridges. No matter which bridge you use, it is important that the shaft of the cue stick does not wobble during your stroke."

ALLEN HOPKINS

"There are a lot of different bridges, but the two basic ones are the open bridge and closed bridge. I recommend the closed bridge, which is the index finger wrapped around the shaft and the other three fingers spread out on the table. The thumb connects with the index finger firmly but not tight. You must feel comfortable and develop a rhythm with your stroke and bridge. Try moving your wrist up higher from the table; it might help you feel more comfortable.''

MIKE SIGEL
"Your bridges should all be solid but have enough room to move freely when stroking. You see many professionals shoot with an open bridge on easier shots, but they already have a grooved stroke! Starting out, try using the standard closed bridge with your index finger around the shaft for added stability.''

EARL STRICKLAND
"For the conventional closed bridge, most people keep the knuckle by the fingernail on the index finger locked. The closed-loop bridge is when the knuckle is bent. There are only a few players besides myself who use the closed-loop bridge. With the knuckle bent, it opens up the hold and has less friction from the cue stick. This bridge, which I use when I am jacked up on the rail, has helped me out of a lot of tough situations.''

KIM DAVENPORT
"On draw shots, I like to use the closed bridge, and on follow shots, the open-hand bridge.''

BUDDY HALL
"With your fingers spread properly, whatever is a comfortable

distance for you, your forefinger, thumb, and index finger should all touch if you are using a closed bridge.''

STROKE

KIM DAVENPORT
''I like to let my stroke out. What I mean by this is that I use a long stroke and follow through.''

EARL STRICKLAND
''If you stroke too many times, it will get you out of rhythm. You stroke no more than four times on any shot. It is important to have a nice fluid stroke.''

MIKE SIGEL
''Your stroke should move back and forth evenly. Try to stroke the same speed you intend to hit the shot with. Shorter shots should be stroked easier and with not as long a stroke. Shots that need to be harder should be stroked either a little faster or with longer strokes.''

ALLEN HOPKINS
''The stroke is very important to practice and develop, if you

want to be a top player. Everybody has his or her own type of stroke, so you have to know your own stroke to determine how you play the game. I practice long, straight-in shots, which helps my follow through and my accuracy. If you are missing straight-in shots, then you have a flaw in your stroke and you will have to work it out with practice. Every top player has this flaw once in a while, and that is one reason they play badly. Usually it's because they haven't been playing or practicing.''

JIM REMPE

''When you are standing over the shot and your tip is just about in contact with the cue ball, your stroking arm should have the elbow straight up and down to the hand. This is probably the single most important basic in pool.''

NICK VARNER

''One of the most important factors on the stroke is the follow through. After contacting the cue ball, let the cue stick go through the cue ball, coming to a natural stop. It varies how far the cue stick goes through the cue ball, depending on the speed of the shot. Normal follow through distance is 4 to 6 inches.''

BUDDY HALL

''I am the only pro that I see who brings the cue tip all the way back through my fingers. I would advise people to come back as far as your back swing would allow you to, in order to get a nice, clean stroke, and even to hesitate instead of using a pendulum motion. Then come straight through, giving the full effect of a full, clean stroke.''

PRACTICE DRILLS

NICK VARNER
"If practicing for Nine Ball tournaments, I practice tough shots, rail shots, break shots, and running-out racks for patter play.''

JIM REMPE
"If you are a beginner, practice shooting with either high, low, or center cue-ball english before you experiment with any side english.''

ALLEN HOPKINS
"For the beginner, I would say to practice your stroke techniques—which is straight-in shots, hitting the cue ball easy and hard. Better players should practice hitting balls very thin and also spinning the cue ball. Shoot the same shots with different english each time.''

MIKE SIGEL
"Normally, if I play Nine Ball I practice tougher parts of the game. Longer shots and the break. In straight pool, I practice running balls and concentrate on patterns that you easily forget when you don't play a lot of straight pool.''

EARL STRICKLAND

"I learned to play by throwing the balls on the table and trying to run out Nine Ball. If I missed, I started over. Beginners should set easy shots or patterns, and as you advance, make them harder."

BUDDY HALL

"I practice Nine Ball by throwing all nine balls on the table and giving myself a simple shot on the one ball, then go as far as I can go. When I miss, I throw them all out there again and start over. I always give myself a simple shot on the one ball and leave the other balls open."

OTHER COMMENTS

JIM REMPE

"Try to get some lessons from a pro, but only listen to one person. Buy some instructional tapes. I recommend "Pool School and Power Pool."

ALLEN HOPKINS

"Once you have decided to start playing pool, you should buy your own cue. The reason I say this is because when you practice with your own cue, you learn what you can do with it. Every cue responds differently to every person's stroke—especially when you use english! You may buy several cues before you find the right one, but when you do, your game will improve more rapidly. Most top players play with the same type of cue their whole life!''

KIM DAVENPORT

''If you want to play pool on the professional level and you think you could make it, don't listen to anyone who says no! Buddy, go and try—but if you try, go all the way!''

EARL STRICKLAND

''When using draw, don't jab at the shot. Most beginners make this mistake. Follow through and aim lower than you think you are going to hit on the cue ball. This helps to maximize your draw. My strength is shot making. Where most people would play a safe, I shoot at it.''

MIKE SIGEL

''The best way to learn the game is to watch better players in your area or buy a good videotape and practice.''

BUDDY HALL

''If you are trying to perform to the top of your ability, you need to make balls. Don't practice tough shots. It's kind of like money: If you watch your *little* money, your *big* money will take care of itself. In other words, if you can make all the simple shots, the hard shots will take care of themselves.''

How to Become a
Touring Professional

(1) Join the MPBA as a PLAYER MEMBER.

(2) Earn eighteen Qualifying Points in REGIONAL events.

(3) Upgrade your membership to SEMI-PRO.

(4) As a Semi-Pro, you can enter Pro Tour events.

(5) Cash in two TOUR events within twelve months.

(6) Upgrade your membership to PROFESSIONAL.

(7) Meet season participation/success requirements.

(8) Upgrade your membership to TOURING PRO.

BECOMING A PLAYER MEMBER

To become a PLAYER MEMBER, contact the:

Professional Billiards Tour Association,
P.O. Box 5599, Spring Hill, FL 34608
904-688-5837
fax 904-686-5515

The PBTA will send you the MPBA PLAYER MEMBER application to complete and return with your annual dues of $25.

Your PLAYER MEMBER card will then be mailed to you. As a PLAYER MEMBER, you can begin earning Qualifying Points on the REGIONAL CIRCUIT.

EARNING QUALIFYING POINTS
ON THE REGIONAL CIRCUIT

The PBTA officially recognizes a REGIONAL CIRCUIT of tournaments held around the country that also serve as qualifying events for PLAYER MEMBERS aspiring to play on the Pro Tour as SEMI-PROFESSIONALS.

The events on the REGIONAL CIRCUIT are open to all players, regardless of MPBA membership (but also allow participation of Semi-Pro, Pro and Touring Pro members). However, only PLAYER MEMBERS earn Qualifying Points.

REGIONAL CIRCUIT tournaments are given three different Class Recognitions by the PBTA:

1. A regular room or local tournament that has no "added" requirement receives its PBTA Recognition as a CLASS A event. When you, as a PLAYER MEMBER, finish in the top half of the field, you are awarded two Qualifying Points by the PBTA.

2. An event with a "minimum added" requirement of $1,000 receives PBTA Recognition as a CLASS AA event. As a PLAYER MEMBER, you receive three Qualifying Points for finishing in the top half of the field.

3. CLASS AAA tournaments require a "minimum added" of $3,000. Six (6) Qualifying Points are awarded for finishing in the top half of the field in AAA events.

Note: The top half of the field means the top half of the tournament chart used, not the top half of the total number of players in the event. Example: If there are twenty-eight players in the event, a thirty-two player chart will be used. Therefore, players finishing in the top sixteen will be awarded points, as opposed to half of the total number of players.

UPGRADING YOUR MEMBERSHIP TO SEMI-PROFESSIONAL

Once you have earned eighteen Qualifying Points on the REGIONAL CIRCUIT (with a minimum of six Qualifying Points obtained in a CLASS AAA recognized event), you can upgrade your MPBA membership from PLAYER MEMBER to SEMI-PROFESSIONAL. The annual dues for SEMI-PROFESSIONAL players are $50 (your $25 PLAYER MEMBER dues are applied to this amount and you are required to pay the additional $25).

Players who have attained SEMI-PRO status, or higher, are also required to execute a Player Agreement with the MPBA, assigning their media and event participation rights to the jurisdiction of the PBTA (see "Player Media and Event Rights").

YOU CAN PLAY ON THE
PRO TOUR

SEMI-PRO players are eligible to enter sanctioned PBTA PRO TOUR events through payment of the required entry fee and adherence to field requirement restrictions and PRO TOUR-governing criteria.

FROM SEMI-PRO TO PRO

A SEMI-PRO must cash (finish in the money) in two (2) PRO TOUR events within a twelve-month period or within ten (10) consecutive PRO TOUR events in order to become eligible for PROFESSIONAL status.

WHAT IS A TOURING PROFESSIONAL?

As a SEMI-PROFESSIONAL or PROFESSIONAL, you begin to earn Tour Ranking Points. The annual dues for a PROFESSIONAL member are $100. (The $50 SEMI-PRO dues previously paid are applied. You are only responsible for paying the $50 difference.)

Professional Players who meet Tour Participation Requirements are awarded TOURING PRO status. As a Touring

Pro, your Ranking becomes valuable toward Selection into limited field events, and for Seeding eligibility in Pro Tour event fields.

Tour Participation Requirements

To be a TOURING PROFESSIONAL, you are required to participate in 50 percent of the scheduled PRO TOUR events each season, including three of the four mandatory events. In addition, you must cash in at least one PRO TOUR event each season.

Seeding and Selection

To remain eligible for Seeding or Selection privileges, players must maintain their TOURING PRO requirements from season to season.

"TOUR NEWS"

Members

As a member of the PBTA/MPBA, you will receive the PBTA periodical newsletter, providing you with the *Tour News* as well as Information, Rankings, and Event Calendars.

Associate Members

Players wishing to associate with and support the Professional Billiards Tour, and who have no aspirations to become professionals, may join as Associate Members. Associate Members are issued a membership card and receive the *Tour News* periodically. Associate Member fees are $25.00 annually.

Pro Tour
Event Information

PLAYER MEDIA AND
PARTICIPATION RIGHTS

SEMI-PRO and TOURING PRO members of the MPBA contract their Participation and Media Rights connected with playing in open tournaments or professional pool competitions to their respective player associations as part of their membership requirements.

Players retain their own Media Rights for all noncompetitive appearances, such as instructional shows, exhibitions, personal appearances, endorsements, commercials, sponsor-related performances, etc.

Players must obtain media releases and/or event releases to perform in nonsanctioned tournaments or other organized pool competitions.

SEMI-PRO, PRO, and TOURING PRO player members are required to contact the PBTA prior to participating in, or signing any contracts that will *obligate* them to participate in, nonsanctioned tournaments or organized competition formats that are not part-recognized or sanctioned by the PBTA.

COMPETITION FORMATS

Tournament formats are set by the PBTA for the various disciplines so that professional play remains consistent for all tournaments. Exceptions for slightly varied formats may be granted to events accommodating larger or smaller fields than the standard 64 players; however, a minimum field of 32 players is required to obtain sanctioning for an event on the Professional Billiards Tour.

NINE BALL:
Nine Ball contests will consist of races to 13 (men) in double-elimination competition requiring a one-set final.

STRAIGHT POOL:
Straight Pool (14.1) contests will be to 150 points in double-elimination competition, with one title match to 200 points.

SEEDING:
Seeding is provided for the top 16 men players in a field of 64 players. When approved fields exceed 64 players, the seeding may be expanded, depending on the overall size of the field and tournament format.

BYE:
Bye positions are designated on the events-pairing chart, prior to the draw, in accordance with the criteria established by the MPBA.

PRIZE FUNDS

One hundred percent of all player entry fees and "added" monies will comprise the total purse in Professional Billiards Tour events. The PBTA will maintain a "Tournament Headquarters Office" at sanctioned professional tournaments. Players that receive cash back or *cashing* but eliminated in early rounds, can collect their winnings at this on-site office.

Prize Fund Distribution will be in accordance with criteria established by the Men's Professional Billiards Association.

ENTRY FEES

You are to remit the required entry fees for sanctioned professional tournaments directly to the PBTA.

GUARANTEED ENTRY FEE PROGRAM

As a PROFESSIONAL or TOURING PROFESSIONAL, you may apply to the MPBA for acceptance into the Guaranteed Entry Program (GEP).

The GEP is a guarantee by the MPBA, on your behalf, for your appearance and entry fee into the Pro Tour event.

THE TOURNAMENT WEEK

(May change for TV, etc.)

DAY ONE

Day one of the five-day tournament week that runs from Wednesday through Sunday (Tuesday through Saturday may be substituted for some events) begins with the players checking into the Tournament hotel (by noon), completing their tournament registration, and preparing for the evening's Opening Festivities.

Press conferences may be arranged by the organizer to boost pre-event publicity. Pro players are to remain available for press photo opportunities.

Title and Support Sponsor hospitality cocktail gatherings may also be scheduled during the evening of Day One by either the PBTA or the organizer of the tournament. Again, players are asked to attend and socialize with the sponsors and their guests. The practice room (Hospitality/Green Room) will be the suggested socialization site and it will double as both the Hospitality area for the Title Sponsor and authorized guests throughout the event. Other than these VIPs, only entered players will be allowed in the Hospitality/Green Room; and only authorized players (those with pending matches) will be allowed on the practice tables.

Player Meeting and Draw: The players' meeting and draw is the official business scheduled for the evening of Day One and it is a requirement that all participants be in attendance. A player/sponsor banquet location or the Tournament Room will be the recommended site for the player meetings and draw.

Day Two
Thursday is when the actual tournament begins, and the competition takes place in both day and evening sessions, continuing over a four-day period. Matches should not begin before noon or after midnight.

Days Three and Four
Friday and Saturday will see the fields begin to narrow as players are eliminated from the double-elimination tournament.

Day Five
Sunday leads us to the finals. The schedule may be formatted to allow the Women's and Men's Finals and Semi-Finals to be staged during different time periods when necessary for television.

CODE OF CONDUCT AND ETHICS

The PBTA honors the Code of Conduct and Ethics established by the Player Association. As a player on the Pro Tour you are an ambassador of the sport. Your demeanor, both in and out of competition, affects the image of your sport and the potential for you and your fellow players to earn a living through professional competition. To enforce the Code of Conduct and Ethics, the MPBA can fine or suspend players that are found to be in violation. A copy of this criteria is available from your player association.

DRESS CODE

Dress Code A: Formal
The Proper dress for men is tuxedo and full vest or cummerbund, with formal or leather shoes.

Dress Code B: Dress
The proper dress will include a jacket to the table with dress pants, dress shirt, or dress sweater or polo, and leather shoes and socks. Slacks with loops must be worn with a belt.

Dress Code C: Casual
The proper dress will include cords, cotton slacks, colored denims, polos, designer shirts, with leather or casual shoes only.

TOURNAMENT AND EVENT ORGANIZERS AND PROMOTERS

Tournament promoters and organizers are offered a variety of benefits when their events are part of the PBTA Tour. Through contracts with organizers for event television rights and titles, the PBTA has the ability to negotiate with TV and corporate sponsors. This generates income for the tour and increases the level of financial return and visibility for the promoters, organizers and their support sponsors.

The PBTA's Regional Circuit Program also enables local tour organizers and proprietors to enhance their events by offering their players the opportunity to earn Qualifying Points. In addition, the sport's professional players, who receive a high level of visibility on the Pro Tour, are eligible to compete in Regional events. Their appearance in your local tournaments affords your regular players the opportunity to compete with the sport's celebrities, and increases the promotional value of your local program.

The PBTA's flexible sanctioning policy makes it possible for room proprietors, professional promoters, commercial enterprises, and independent program producers to coordinate and successfully involve their events with the Pro Tour.

Information for organizers or promoters on PBTA-sanctioned tournaments or events is acquired through the PBTA office.

HOW TO RUN A TOURNAMENT

For information on how to run a tournament, contact the PBTA office. Tournament charts and other tournament supplies will be made available to you.

PBTA
P.O. Box 5599
Spring Hill, FL 34608
904-688-5837
fax 904-686-5515

STATE CHAMPIONSHIP CRITERIA

The PBTA will recognize such events as State Championships only if such events are under the CLASS AAA regional criteria. The event must be sanctioned by the PBTA, and the minimum added to the prize fund by the promoter be $3,000 (men's division) and $1,000 (women's division). There is also a minimum field requirement of 32 (men's division) and 16 (women's division).

What Is the
American Poolplayers Association
(APA)?

The American Poolplayers Association (APA) is the "Governing Body of Amateur Pool" in the United States. Located in Lake St. Louis, Missouri, the APA oversees all aspects of amateur pool, including establishing and administering amateur rules of play, administering the official handicap systems for amateur play, administering the national amateur championships, and sanctioning the nation's largest amateur pool league.

The APA originated in 1979, when Terry Bell and Larry Hubbart, both professional players, developed an idea for a centrally controlled nationwide amateur pool organization. Both men realized how popular the sport of billiards was becoming, but felt the sport lacked an organized recreational amateur system. With a marketplace of over 38 million billiards enthusiasts, they realized they were onto something big.

Based on their knowledge of the game, they developed handicap systems for both Eight Ball and Nine Ball that allow players of all abilities to compete equally. These handicap systems are equally effective for singles and team play. Of all the programs administered by the APA, its 8-Ball League is the most popular. This league, which has Bud Light sponsorship, is nationwide in scope, and in 1992 boasted more than 100,000 participants.

The APA conducts the national amateur championships, and makes available to the amateur player a number of programs including league, tournament, and singles play. There is competition for women only, men only, and mixed, as well as for junior and senior citizens.

APA rules, formats, and handicap systems are recognized and endorsed by the MPBA and the PBTA as the official systems for amateur play in the United States, making the APA the most prestigious amateur entity within the billiards industry.

Anyone interested in more information about amateur play and the American Poolplayers Association should call (314) 625-8611.

General Rules of Pocket Billiards

STANDARD FOULS

Note: Where it is stated that a referee should decide a ruling, and there is not a referee or third person available, the players competing will decide the ruling.

Scratch: Pocketing the cue ball or driving it off the table is a foul.

No rail: If no object ball is pocketed, failure to drive the cue ball or some object ball to a rail after the cue ball contacts the object ball is a foul.

Foot: Failure to have at least one foot in contact with the floor at the moment the cue tip contacts the cue ball is a foul.

Moving ball: Shooting while any ball is moving or spinning is a foul.

Push shot or double stroke: When the cue ball is frozen to an object ball, you may shoot the cue ball in any direction with a level cue and it is legal. If the two balls are *not* frozen, you must elevate your cue stick and the cue ball must slow up with reverse english after striking the object ball (unless you masse the cue ball). This is a delicate shot, and it is advised to have a referee call the shot.

Touched object ball: It is not a foul to accidentally touch stationary object balls while in the act of shooting, but it is a foul if the player shooting attempts to restore the moved object ball before giving the nonshooter the option of placement.

If such an accident occurs, the player should allow the referee or nonshooting player to restore the object balls to their correct positions. At the nonshooting player's option, the disturbed balls will be left in their new positions. In this case, the balls are considered restored, and subsequent contact on them is not a foul.

If a ball set in motion as a normal part of the shot passes partly into a region originally occupied by a disturbed ball, the shot is foul. In short, if the accident has any effect on the outcome of the shot, it is a foul. (Example: Player shooting the cue ball into the one ball moves the three ball accidentally. The cue ball's path then crosses where the three ball used to be, but since the three ball was repositioned, the cue ball and three do not collide.)

It is a foul to play another shot before the referee has restored any accidentally moved balls. It is a foul to touch a moving ball or to allow that ball to hit any foreign object, such as a cube of chalk (the top of the rail is not considered to be a foreign object).

Rail safety: When an object ball is close to a rail but not frozen, and players are taking turns softly tapping the object ball with the cue ball to the same rail, this is called a rail safety. The player who performed this shot first must make the cue ball hit any rail or make the object ball go to a different rail on his third attempt—or it is a foul.

Placement: Touching any object ball with the cue ball while it is in hand is a foul.

Split hit: In very rare circumstances, it is possible for the cue ball to contact two object balls at the same time. This is called a split hit. It is considered a bad hit if one of those balls is supposed to be contacted first. (Example: Playing Nine Ball, the one ball and seven ball were hit at the same time and the referee called a split hit. Since the one ball must be contacted first, it is considered a bad hit. Playing Eight Ball, the shooter has stripes, hits a solid and striped ball at the same time. This is a bad hit, since he must contact his striped ball first.)

Object ball: Players may touch object balls only to assist the referee in his duties. If a player intentionally touches any object ball for any other purpose while a game is in progress—whether that object ball is in play or not—he has fouled. (This rule does not apply in the touched-object-ball situation.)

Cue ball: Except for ball-in-hand placement, if a player touches the cue ball with anything other than the chalked surface of his cue tip, he has fouled whether the cue ball moves or not. The player may place the cue ball (as in ball-in-hand) with anything other than the chalked surface of his cue tip.

Scoop shot: If a player plays a shot with extreme draw with the intention of miscuing to make the cue ball jump over some obstruction, he has fouled. (See ''Jump Shots.'') Any miscue when executing a jump shot is a foul.

Interference: If the nonshooting player distracts his opponent or interferes with his play, he has fouled. If a player shoots out of turn, or moves any ball except during his inning, it is considered to be interference.

Devices: Using any device in an uncustomary manner in lining up or executing a shot is a foul.

Practice: While a game is in progress, practice is not allowed. Taking a shot that is not part of that game is a foul.

Ball off the table: While, during a shot, the cue ball or any object ball lands off the playing surface, it is a foul.

SERIOUS FOULS

The following serious fouls are penalized by the loss of one game, if the referee has warned the player before the foul. If the referee fails to warn the player, any foul is penalized like a standard foul, except as noted.

Three consecutive fouls: If a player fouls three times without making an intervening legal shot, he loses the game. The three fouls must occur in one game. The warning must be given between the second and third fouls. If the warning is not given and the shooter makes his third foul, it is not loss of game and that shooter is back ''on two'' fouls. At this point, he still must be notified that he has two fouls.

Assistance: While a match is in progress, players are not allowed to ask spectators for assistance in planning or executing shots. If a player asks for and receives such assistance, he loses the game. (In 14.1 a player who asks for assistance will lose his turn at the table and receive a foul) Any spectator who spontaneously offers any significant help to a player will be removed from the area. (See ''Outside Interference.'')

Failure to leave the table: If a player does not stop shooting as soon as the referee has called a foul, he loses the game. The calling of the foul is considered to be the referee's warning to the player.

Slow play: If the referee feels a player is playing exceptionally slow, he must warn the player that he risks loss of a game if such slow play continues. Subsequently, if the referee and the tournament director agree that his play remains unacceptably slow, they may penalize the player one game for each game in which such slow play continues. (In general, no shot should take more than two minutes to plan and execute.)

Head string: If, after a scratch on a break shot, the cue ball is in hand below the head string (as in 14.1 and ''One Pocket''),the referee should say, ''Below the head string,'' when he hands the cue ball to the player—which constitutes the warning. If the player intentionally places the cue ball above the head string, he loses the game. If the player accidentally places the cue ball slightly above the head string, the referee must warn him again, or no foul is considered to have occurred. With cue ball in hand below the head string, if the player plays directly on an object ball below the head string without the cue ball first crossing it, he loses the game. No warning is required in this last case.

Suspended play: If a player shoots while play is suspended by the referee, he loses the game. Announcement of the suspension is considered sufficient warning.

Concession: If a player concedes, he loses the game. The unscrewing of a jointed cue stick, except to replace a shaft, is considered to be a concession. The player must notify his opponent prior to replacing a shaft. No warning from the referee is required in the case of a concession.

OTHER SITUATIONS AND INTERPRETATIONS

Outside interference: When outside interference occurs during a shot that has an effect on the outcome of that shot, the referee will restore the balls to the positions they had before the shot, and the shot will be replayed. If the interference had no effect on the shot, the referee will restore the disturbed balls and play will continue.

Settling into place: A ball may settle slightly after it appears to have stopped, possibly due to slight imperfections in the ball or the table. Unless this causes a ball to fall into a pocket, it is considered a normal hazard of play, and the ball will not be moved back. If a ball falls into a pocket as the result of such settling, it is replaced as close as possible to its original position. If a ball falls into a pocket during or just prior to a shot, and has an effect on the shot, the referee will restore the position and the shot will be replayed. Players are not penalized for shooting while a ball is settling.

Jump shots: It is legal to cause the cue ball to rise off the bed of the table by elevating the cue stick on the shot, and forcing the cue ball to rebound from the bed of the table. It is not legal to scoop under the cue ball with the intention of lifting the cue ball over the obstruction; this is a foul. A miscue on a jump shot is a foul.

Protesting fouls: If a player thinks that the referee has failed to call a foul, he must protest to the referee before the next shot starts. If he fails to do so, and the foul goes unpenalized, the foul is considered not to have occurred. The referee is the final judge on matters of fact. If either player thinks that the referee is applying the rules incorrectly, and the dispute cannot be resolved by reference to the rules, the referee must take the protest to the tournament director or his appointed substitute. The tournament director's decision on interpretation of the rules is final. A player may also protest if he thinks that the referee has called a foul incorrectly. In any case, play is suspended until the protest is resolved.

Prompting warnings: When a player thinks that the referee is failing to issue a mandatory warning, he may remind the referee that such a warning is necessary.

Waiving specific rules: Prior to the start of the tournament, the tournament director may choose to waive or modify specific rules; e.g., the loser of a game rather than the winner may break the following games.

Late start: A player must be ready to begin a match within fifteen minutes of the start of the match, or his opponent wins by forfeit. The starting time is considered to be the scheduled time or the time the match is announced, whichever is later.

Unsportsmanlike conduct: If the referee and the tournament director agree that a player is persistently behaving in a disruptive or unsportsmanlike manner, they may penalize him in any way they choose, including calling a foul on him, awarding the game or match to his opponent, or forfeiting all of his remaining matches.

INSTRUCTIONS FOR THE REFEREE

The referee will maintain order and enforce these rules. He is the final judge in all matters of fact. His duties include, but are not limited to, the following:

Before the match: Before the match, the referee will clean the table and balls, if necessary. He will ensure that chalk and mechanical bridges are available. He will mark the head string and long string with a pencil, if they are not already marked.

Racking: The referee will rack the balls as tightly as possible—which means that each ball should be touching its neighbors. Tapping a ball into place is not recommended. Also, it is preferable to thoroughly brush the area of the rack to even out the cloth.

Calling fouls: The referee will call fouls as soon as they occur and will inform the incoming player that he has ball in hand.

Clearing pockets: On tables that do not have ball-return systems, the referee will remove pocketed object balls from full or nearly full pockets. It is the player's responsibility to see that this duty is performed; he has no recourse if a ball rebounds from a full pocket.

Cleaning balls: During a game, a player may ask the referee to clean one or more balls. The referee will clean any visibly soiled ball.

Soliciting information: If the referee does not have a clear view of a possible foul, he may ask spectators for assistance in determining what occurred. The referee will then weigh all evidence as he sees fit.

Warnings that are mandatory: The referee must warn a player who is about to commit a serious foul, otherwise any foul is considered to be a standard foul (except as specially noted). The referee must warn a player who has had two consecutive fouls, otherwise the player is considered to have had only one foul prior to the shot. The referee must warn a player when an object ball is touching a rail, otherwise any contact on that ball is considered to have driven it to that rail. The referee should issue warnings as soon as the corresponding situation arises. A warning given just as a shot starts is not considered sufficient; the player must be given enough time to react.

Restoring a position: When it becomes necessary, the referee will restore disturbed balls to their original positions, to the best of his ability. The referee may ask for information for this purpose if he is not sure of their original positions. If the balls were disturbed by one player, the other player has the option of preventing the restoration. In this case, the referee should clearly indicate where the balls will be moved to if they are restored, and only restore the balls if requested to do so.

Advice and rules clarifications: The referee must not give advice to the players on points of play except to clarify the rules. When asked for such clarification, the referee will explain the applicable rules to the best of his ability, but any misstatement by the referee will not protect a player from enforcement of the actual rules. When asked, the referee must tell a player how many consecutive fouls have been committed, what the score is, whether the cue ball is touching an object ball, what the restored position would be, etc.

Suspending play: The referee has the authority to suspend play during protests by players and whenever he feels that conditions are unsuitable for play to continue. If a spectator is interfering with the game, play may be suspended until that spectator is removed from the area.

PLAYING WITHOUT A REFEREE

It is the responsibility of the player who is not at the table to get a third person when there is a shot that comes up that may lead to controversy. If a third person is not called in, it is the shooter who is awarded the decision. The nonshooting player must notify the shooter to stop play until that third person is available. If the shooter is notified to stop play and he continues shooting, he loses the game.

Third opinion: When a shot comes up that seems likely to lead to controversy, a third person should be temporarily enlisted to provide a third opinion.

Resolving disputes: Any dispute between the two players will be resolved by the tournament director or his appointed substitute.

Terms and Definitions

Following are some billiards terms and their definitions:

Shot: A shot begins at the instant the cue tip contacts the cue ball, and ends when all balls in play stop rolling and spinning. (See Section 9.3.)

Inning: A player's inning begins when it is legal for him to take a shot and ends at the end of a shot on which he misses, fouls, or wins, or when he fouls between shots.

Game: A game starts when the referee has finished racking the balls, and ends at the end of a legal shot that pockets the nine or when a player forfeits the game as the result of a foul.

Match: A match starts when the players are ready to lag, and ends when the deciding game ends.

Above/Below the head string: A ball is below the head string if its center is below the head string (toward the head end of the table). A ball is above the head string if its center is above the head string (toward the foot or rack end of the table).

Stopped ball that falls: A ball resting on the brink of a pocket is considered to have stopped if as determined by the referee, it remains motionless for five seconds. If any player or spectator causes such a ball to fall in before the five-second limit by bumping or otherwise moving the table, the ball will be replaced at the edge of the pocket and is not considered pocketed. The time begins when all other balls have stopped and the shot ends at the end of the five seconds.

Base of ball: In a situation where players must determine whether the object ball is above or below the head string, it is the base of the ball (the portion of ball contacting the playing surface) that determines this.

Pocketed: A ball is considered pocketed when it comes to rest in a pocket or enters the ball-return system of the table. A ball that hits the lining of the pocket or another ball already in the pocket, and returns to the surface of the table or jumps off the table, is not considered pocketed. If a ball comes to rest at the brink of a pocket so that it is partly supported by another ball, it is considered to be pocketed if the removal of the supporting ball would cause the supported ball to fall into the pocket.

To a rail: A ball is driven to a rail if it is not touching a rail, and then touches a rail. A ball that is touching a rail at the start of a shot and then is forced into the same rail is not considered to have been driven to that rail unless it leaves the rail and returns. A ball is considered to have been driven to a rail if it touches the pocket back or facing.

Spotting balls: All object balls that have been pocketed illegally or driven off the table are spotted by the referee after the shot is over. Object balls are spotted by placing them on the long string—on or below the foot spot if possible, and as close to the foot spot as possible. This does not apply to Nine Ball or Eight Ball since all balls pocketed or driven off the table stay down.

Frozen object ball: When a player chooses to shoot an object ball that is frozen to a rail, the player must either pocket that object ball or any other ball; or drive the frozen object ball to a different rail; or, after hitting the frozen object ball, drive the cue ball to any rail; or drive any other object ball to a rail; or drive the frozen object ball into another object ball and hit any rail with either object ball.

Ball in hand: When the cue ball is in hand, the player may place the cue ball anywhere on the bed of the table, except in contact with an object ball (this would be a foul). He may continue to adjust the position of the cue ball until he takes a shot. With ball in hand below the head string (after a scratch on the break in 14.1 and One Pocket), the player may not place the cue ball above the head string.

Ball off the table: An unpocketed ball is considered to be driven off the table if it comes to rest other than on the bed of the table. It is a foul to drive an object ball off the table. In Nine Ball and Eight Ball, the ball driven off the table will stay down; in One Pocket and 14.1, the ball will be spotted.

Miscue: A miscue occurs when the tip of the cue stick slides off the cue ball due to insufficient chalk or to a contact point too far from center. It is usually accompanied by a sharp sound and a departure of the cue ball from its expected line of travel.

Lag: Players lag by shooting at the same time from behind the head string to contact the foot rail and then have the cue ball come to rest as close as possible to the head rail. Object balls may be substituted if two cue balls are not available. A player loses the lag if his cue ball is pocketed or driven off the table. Ties are replayed. The distance from the cue ball to the head rail is the shortest distance between the cue ball and any cloth-covered part of the rail (the cushion nose of the pocket facing).

Push out: The player who shoots the shot immediately after a legal break may play a push out. On a push out, the cue ball is not required to contact any object ball or any rail, so through Rules in section 3.2, 4.1, 4.2 of 9 balls are suspended; but all other foul rules still apply. The player must announce his intention of playing a push out before the shot, or the shot is considered to be a normal shot. Any ball pocketed on a push out does not count and is spotted. Following a legal push out, the incoming player is permitted to shoot from that position or to pass the shot back to the player who pushed out. A push out is not considered to be a foul as long as no rule (except 4.2 or 4) is violated. An illegal push out is penalized according to the type of foul committed

Bank shot: When the object ball contacts one or more rails before being pocketed. This does not include when the object ball rides along the rail before being pocketed. Example: "You must bank the eight ball."

Cluster: When two or more object balls are touching or near each other on the table. Example: "I will attempt to break apart

Kick shot: When the cue ball comes behind the object ball to make the hit. Example: "The only thing he could do was play a kick shot."

Draw shot: This is done when striking the cue ball below the center to put reverse english on it in attempts to bring the cue ball in a backward motion after striking the object ball. It is usually done for position play. Example: "He had to draw the cue ball back to get position on the two ball."

Follow: This is done when striking the cue ball above the center to put forward spin on it in attempts to move the cue ball forward after striking the object ball. Is usually done for position play. Example: "He had to put follow on the cue ball in order to get position on the five ball."

Left-hand english: This is done when striking the cue ball left of the cue ball's center, and is done for position play or sometimes to throw an object ball into a pocket. Example: "He used left-hand english to help pocket the six ball on the tough cut shot."

Right-hand english: This is done when striking the cue ball right of the cue ball's center, and is done for position play or sometimes to throw an object ball into a pocket. Example: "Right-hand english made it easier to get the cue ball to the other end of the table."

Kiss shot: When the object ball or cue ball makes contact with a ball more than once during a shot. Example: "He pocketed the one ball by playing a kiss shot off the seven ball."

Combination: Shooting the cue ball into an object ball that strikes one or more other object balls to pocket a ball. Example: "He played the one-nine combination to win the game."

Tangent line: When two balls are frozen together, there is an imaginary line that runs between them. Knowing about this and how to use it helps to pocket balls that normally would be too difficult to make. Example: "Using the tangent line, he figured out how to pocket the twelve ball to keep his run in straight pool going."

Object ball: Balls other than the cue ball in a game of pocket billiards.

Masse: When raising the butt of your cue stick and striking down on one side of the cue ball with a certain stroke, the cue ball takes a curved path. It is usually done when a player needs the cue ball to go around an object ball to strike a different object ball. Example: "Because the six ball was blocking the cue ball's path to make a good hit on the two ball, he had to masse the cue ball."

Inside english: If you apply side spin on the same side of the cue ball that is the direction of the cue ball's normal path without english, this is inside english. In other words, if the cue ball's normal path without any english would be traveling to the left after striking the object ball, left-hand english would be inside english. Example: "He used inside english to make the cue ball move faster around the table."

Outside english: If you apply side spin on the opposite side of the cue ball from the direction of the cue ball's normal path without english, this is outside english. In other words, if the cue ball's normal path without any english would be traveling to the left after striking the object ball, right-hand english would be outside english. Example: "He used outside english to make the cue ball move the least amount possible."

Leave: The position of the balls on the table you are left with after your opponent's turn at the table. Example: "The leave after his opponent finished shooting was not a good one."

Split hit: When the cue ball strikes two object balls at precisely the same time (see the General Rules section). Example: "The referee called a split hit, and since they were playing Nine Ball, it was considered a bad hit."

Corner-hooked: When the cue ball rests on the edge of the pocket so that the cushion is in the way of the player contacting the object ball. Example: "Because I was corner-hooked, I had to kick at the object ball."

On the hill: When a player only needs one game or ball to win the match. Example: "With the score being six-to-four in a race to seven, he was on the hill."

To the wire: This is when both players need only one game or ball to win the match. Example: "The match went to the wire, since the score was six-to-six in a race to seven."

Hooked: When the cue ball does not have a clear path to the object ball that the player would like to contact (see also "Snookered"). Example: "After missing the two ball, my opponent left me hooked without a shot."

Run out: When a player clears all the object balls needed to win the game or match without missing. Example: "A good player will run out almost every time he gets to an open table."

Snookered: When the cue ball does not have a clear path to the object ball that the player would like to contact (see also "Hooked"). Example: "He was snookered behind the five ball."

Carom: When a ball is played off of another ball. Example: "He caromed the cue ball off the seven ball to pocket the three ball."

Flip: In the professional tournaments, the players always lag to see who will have choice of break; but occasionally, outside of professional play, the flip of a coin determines the winner of the break. Example: "The two players flipped for the break."

Stop shot: This is done when the cue ball stops as soon as it makes contact with the object ball. Example: "He needed to play a stop shot to get position for his next ball."

Follow through: When the tip of the cue stick passes through the spot where the cue ball was before striking it. Example: "You should follow through on every shot."

Match: A predetermined number of games or points that a player must reach to win constitutes a match. Example: "During the match the players executed many amazing shots."

Bridge (mechanical bridge): An aide in helping players when they need to execute a shot that is too far for them to shoot comfortably. Example: "Once you learn to use the bridge correctly, it will improve your game."

Bridge hand: This is the hand a shooter would use to rest the cue stick on and guide the cue stick during a shot. Example: "His bridge hand looked very solid."

Diamond system: A system used by players to help determine a ball's path during the shot. This system includes markings to go by that are permanently set into the rails. Example: "His knowledge of the diamond system showed when he used it to kick at the ball."

Cross side/corner: This is when the object ball is banked either into the side pocket or corner pocket. Example: "I will play the eight ball cross side."

Inning: A player's inning begins when he first strikes the cue ball and ends when he fails to pocket an object ball. Example: "During his inning at the table, he ran three racks."

Rail: See diagram #1.

Cushion: The clothed rubber portion of the table that surrounds the playing surface. Example: "He drove the object ball to the cushion."

Cloth: This is the material that covers the playing surface and cushions. Example: "He was used to playing on fast cloth."

Key ball: This is the shot during a game that is usually the most difficult to perform. It may also be the shot prior to the break shot in straight pool. Example: "The key ball in that game was the three ball."

Seeding: During a tournament format, players may be seeded on the tournament chart. This means that a certain amount of top-ranked players are placed into the chart slots prior to the start of the tournament. This saves seeded players from scrambling for places. It is one of the advantages to being in the top of the tour rankings. Example: "He was the number three seed."

Stroke: The back-and-forth motion of the cue stick as a player executes a shot. Example: "His stroke was smooth as he shot the ball."

Safety: This is a defensive type of shot, and if executed correctly, one that makes it difficult on the incoming player. Example: "He chose to play a safety, since the ball was too difficult to pocket."

Object ball: During a game, the object ball is the ball other than the cue ball. Example: "He only needed to pocket one more object ball to win the game."

Miscue: This is when the tip of the cue stick slides off the cue ball, not giving it the desired contact. Example: "Because he did not chalk his tip, this caused a miscue."

Race: A predetermined number of games is set, and the first player to reach that number wins the race. See also match. Example: "They played a race to eleven."

Double elimination: This is a format in which a player would be eliminated from the event if he lost two matches.

Single elimination: This is a format in which a player would be eliminated from the event if he lost one match.

Playing surface: This is considered the clothed, flat surface that is surrounded by the cushions, but it does not include the cushions or rails.

Billiards Rules of Play

NINE BALL

1. Summary

Nine Ball is played with nine object balls numbered one through nine and a cue ball. On each shot, the first ball the cue ball contacts must be the lowest-numbered ball on the table, but the balls do not need to be pocketed in order. If a player pockets any ball on a legal shot, he remains at the table for another shot, and continues until he misses, fouls, or wins the game by pocketing the nine ball. After a miss, the incoming player must shoot from the position left by the previous player, but after a foul the incoming player may start with the cue ball anywhere on the table. Certain serious fouls are penalized by loss of the game. Players are not required to call any shot. A match ends when one of the players has won the required number of games.

2. Beginning Play

2.1 ORDER OF PLAY.
Order of play for the first game is determined by lag. The winner of the lag may break the first rack or assign the break to his opponent. In subsequent games of the match, the winner of the previous game will have the option to break.

2.2 RACKING THE BALLS
The object balls are racked in a diamond shape, with the one ball

at the top of the diamond and on the foot spot, the nine ball in the center of the diamond, and the other balls in arbitrary order, as shown. If the one ball is not touching both of the adjacent balls, the breaker may ask the referee to re-rack the balls prior to the break. The cue ball begins in hand behind the head string.

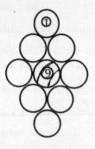

Diagram #2

2.3 BREAK SHOT
The rules governing the break shot are the same as for other shots except that:

(a) If the cue ball is pocketed or driven off the table, the incoming player has the cue ball in hand anywhere on the table and all balls pocketed will stay down, except the nine ball—in which case it will be spotted.

(b) The breaker must attempt an ''open break''; that is, he must attempt to pocket a ball. Failure to do so is a standard foul.

(c) If the shooter attempts an open break and the cue ball crosses the head string but fails to contact the one ball first, this is considered a foul. The balls are re-racked and the incoming player may break or assign the break back to his opponent.

(d) On the shot immediately following a legal break, the shooter may play a "push out" (see "Push Out" in the General Rules section).

3. Continuing Play

3.1 AFTER THE BREAK
If the breaker pockets one or more balls on a legal break, he continues to shoot until he misses, fouls, or wins the game. If the player misses or fouls, the other player begins his inning and shoots until he misses, fouls, or wins. The game ends when the nine ball is pocketed on a legal shot, or the game is forfeited for a serious infraction of the rules.

3.2 BALL TO A RAIL
After contacting the lowest-numbered ball on the table first, any object ball or the cue ball must be driven to a rail or the shot is foul and incoming player has ball in hand.

3.3 SAFETIES
A player may shoot a safety shot instead of attempting to pocket an object ball. This is usually done when it is not likely or possible to pocket an object ball. A player does not have to call a

safety. A player's turn at the table ends after he has executed an attempted safety.

3.4 WINNING
A player has won the game when he legally pockets the nine ball.

4. Standard Fouls

When a player commits a standard foul (see "Standard Fouls" in the General Rules section), he must relinquish his run at the table. All balls pocketed on the foul will stay down except the nine ball, which is spotted. The incoming player is awarded ball in hand; prior to his first shot, he may place the cue ball anywhere on the table. If a player fouls during the other player's inning, the shooter is awarded ball in hand, and if the foul had an effect on the position of the balls, the referee will restore the position if requested to do so by the shooter. If a player commits several standard fouls on one shot, they are counted as only one foul.

4.1 BAD HIT
If the first object ball contacted by the cue ball is not the lowest-numbered ball on the table, the shot is foul.

4.2 SPLIT HIT
If the cue ball strikes two object balls at the same instant and the

referee calls a split hit, it is a foul. The lowest ball on the table must be the only object ball to be contacted first.

Note: Where it is stated that a referee should decide a ruling, and there is not a referee or third person available, the players competing will decide the ruling.

ONE POCKET

1. Summary
The object of One Pocket is to pocket eight of the fifteen balls before your opponent does. You may use only one of the two scoring pockets, which are the corner pockets located at the foot of the table. This constitutes one game. It is common in professional play that the first player to win five games is the winner of the match.

2. Beginning Play

2.1 ORDER OF PLAY
Players lag for the choice of break. Winner of the lag has an option of breaking or letting his opponent break. The breaker will then choose one of the two scoring pockets to use during the entire game and his opponent has the other pocket for scoring.

2.2 RACKING THE BALLS

The fifteen object balls are racked in a triangle on the foot spot as shown. All fifteen object balls may be placed randomly in the rack.

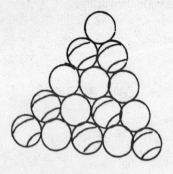

Diagram #3

2.3 BREAK SHOT

To constitute a legal break, the player must either contact an object ball with the cue ball and drive at least one object ball or cue ball to a rail, or pocket an object ball into his scoring pocket. Failure to do this is a foul.

3. Scoring

A point is scored when an object ball is legally pocketed in the shooter's scoring pocket. Players do not have to call their shot. If the shooter pockets an object ball in his opponent's scoring pocket, his opponent keeps the point and the shooter loses his turn at the table. If legally pocketing a ball in the opponent's scoring pocket brings the opponent's score to the amount needed to win the game, then the shooter has lost.

The only time a point is not counted after pocketing an object ball in a scoring pocket is when the shooter scratches the cue ball at the same time. If this happens, the object ball is then spotted on the foot spot (see "Spotting Balls" in the General Rules section) and the shooter loses his turn at the table. In this situation, the shooter is also penalized an additional point and that ball is spotted before his opponent's turn at the table.

4. RULES OF PLAY
To constitute a legal shot, the shooter must either pocket any object ball, or, with the cue ball, drive any object ball to a rail, or drive the cue ball to a rail after contacting any object ball.

5.STANDARD FOULS
Any time the shooter commits a foul, he loses his turn at the table and is penalized a point. One of his previously scored object balls is spotted. If he does not have an object ball to spot, he owes one. The next time he legally scores, his scored object ball is spotted at the end of that inning. If a player commits three consecutive fouls, it is loss of game for that player. (See "Three Scratch Rule" in the General Rules section.)

5.1 SCRATCH
If a player pockets the cue ball or drives the cue ball off the table, it is considered a foul. His opponent then has ball in hand

behind the head string. If all of the object balls are behind the head string, the shooter has the option to spot, on the foot spot, the ball closest to the head string. If two or more object balls behind the head string are the at the same distance from and closest to the head string, the shooter may choose which of them he would like spotted.

5.2 ILLEGALLY POCKETED BALLS

Object balls that are pocketed in the four nonscoring pockets are illegally pocketed balls. The shooter loses his turn and the object ball is spotted. The shooter is not penalized for this. If the shooter makes a legal shot and sinks a ball in his pocket at the same time pockets a ball in a nonscoring pocket, the shooter continues his turn at the table and the illegally pocketed ball is spotted at the end of his inning. If the shooter pockets the last object ball on the table and needs that illegally pocketed ball being held to win the game, the ball is spotted and the player continues to shoot.

5.3 DOUBLE-HIT CUE BALL

If at any time during the game the cue ball is hit twice during one shot, it is a foul. The incoming player has the option of taking the shot as is, or having ball in hand behind the headstring.

6. ALTERNATE BREAKS

In tournament play, there is usually more than one game played to constitute a match. Therefore, the loser of the previous game will be the breaker of the new game.

Note: Where it is stated that a referee should decide a ruling, and there is not a referee or third person available, the players competing will decide the ruling.

STRAIGHT POOL
(14.1)

1. Summary

The game of straight pool, or 14.1 Continuous, is played with a cue ball and all fifteen object balls. The object is to consecutively pocket balls until you reach the amount of points that are designated before the game begins. Professional games are usually played to 150 points. A point is scored when an object ball is legally pocketed.

2. Beginning Play

2.1 ORDER OF PLAY

Order of play is determined by lag. Winner of the lag has an option to break or let his opponent break.

2.2 RACKING THE BALLS

The fifteen object balls are racked in a triangle on the foot spot as shown. They may be placed randomly in the rack.

Diagram #4

2.3 OPENING BREAK

The breaker has ball in hand behind the head string. With the cue ball, the player who breaks must either drive two or more object balls and the cue ball to a rail or pocket an object ball in a predetermined pocket.

If a legal break is not accomplished and the shooter does not scratch, he is charged a two-point penalty and his score is "minus two." This is a breaking foul. It is then the opponent's choice to shoot the balls as they lay, or he may have the balls re-racked and have his opponent break again.

If the breaker does not drive two balls to a rail, and scratches, the opponent has ball in hand behind the head string and may shoot the balls as they lay, or he may have the balls re-racked and have his opponent break again. Each time the opening break is not successfully executed, the breaker is penalized two points. The three-consecutive-foul rule does not apply in the opening break.

If the breaker drives two object balls to the rail, but

scratches, he is only penalized one point. The incoming player then has ball in hand behind the head string. The consecutive foul rule does apply in this situation.

2.4 SCORING POINTS

A player scores a point when he legally pockets an object ball into a predetermined pocket. It does not matter how that ball reaches the pocket, the player only needs to designate which ball and which pocket. If any other ball is pocketed in the same stroke, the player receives that point too. As long as the shooter scores a point, he continues at the table until he fails to legally pocket a ball. It is then the incoming player's turn at the table.

After the fourteenth ball is pocketed and there is only one object ball and the cue ball left on the table, the fourteen balls are then racked as shown with the space in the rack at the foot spot. The player at the table continues shooting. The object at this point is to pocket the fifteenth ball and use the cue ball to spread apart the fourteen racked balls. This will enable the shooter to continue his run if done properly.

When racking the fourteen object balls, if the cue ball or the fifteenth ball is in the way of the rack, the chart below will tell you what to do depending on the situation.

15th Ball Lies \ Cue Ball Lies	In the rack	Not in the rack and not in the head spot	On the head spot*
In the rack	15th ball - foot spot Cue-in kitchen	15th ball - head spot Cue-in position	15th ball - center spot
Pocketed	15th ball - foot spot Cue-in kitchen	15th ball - foot spot Cue-in position	15th ball - foot spot Cue-in position
In the kitchen and not on the head spot	15th ball - in position Cue-head spot	X	X
Not in the kitchen and not on the rack	15th ball - in position Cue-in kitchen	X	X *
On the head spot	15th ball - in position Cue-center spot	X	X

*On-head spot means to interfere with spotting a ball on a head spot.

Diagram #5

2.5 SAFETIES

A player may shoot a safety shot instead of attempting to pocket an object ball. This is usually done when it is not likely or possible to pocket an object ball. A player does not have to call a safety. A player's turn at the table ends after he has executed an attempted safety. When an object ball is pocketed during a safety, it is spotted on the foot spot and the cue ball remains in place.

There are times in safe play when an object ball close to

a rail is lightly tapped into the rail with the cue ball to leave the opponent with a similar shot. Players are allowed to do this two times each. On the third attempt, the frozen rule applies. If a player fails to execute this correctly on the third attempt, the incoming player has the option to take ball in hand behind the head string, with all object balls staying in position, or have his opponent make an opening break.

2.6 ILLEGALLY POCKETED BALLS
When an object ball is illegally pocketed, the object ball is spotted. This is not a foul.

2.7 MISSES
When a player does not pocket an object ball that is called, it is not a foul. The cue ball must, however, contact a rail or drive any object ball to a rail after striking any object ball. Failure to do this at any time is a foul.

3. Penalties for Fouls

Each time a foul is committed, the player committing the foul is penalized one point. This will be deducted from his score. If a player commits three consecutive fouls, he will then be penalized fifteen points in addition to the three points already penalized. Three consecutive fouls means that for three consecutive turns at the table a player, on his first shot of the inning, commits a foul. Once the fifteen-ball penalty is given, all fouls on that player are cleared, the incoming player has the option to take the table as is or re-rack the balls and have his opponent make an opening break.

3.1 JUMPED BALL

If an object ball lays to rest off the playing surface (see "Playing Surface" in general rules), it is a foul. A one-point penalty is assessed and the jumped ball and any balls pocketed during the same shot are spotted. A player does not receive any points for pocketed balls during a jumped ball shot.

3.2 FOULS ON ALL BALLS

If at any time a player touches the cue ball or any other object ball, it is a foul and a one-point penalty is assessed.

3.3 BALL IN HAND BEHIND HEAD STRING

When a player has ball in hand behind the head string and all object balls are also behind the head string, the shooter has the option to spot the object ball closest to the head string on the foot spot. If there are two or more object balls at the same distance from and closest to the head string, the player has his choice of one to spot on the foot spot.

3.4 DOUBLE-HIT CUE

If at any time during the game the cue ball is hit twice during one shot, it is a foul. The incoming player has the option of taking the shot as is, or having ball in hand behind the headstring.

Note: Where it is stated that a referee should decide a ruling, and there is not a referee or third person available, the players competing will decide the ruling.

TEN BALL

1. Summary

Ten Ball is played with ten object balls, numbered one through ten, and a cue ball. It is played exactly the same as Nine Ball is played (see Nine Ball rules).

2. Racking the Balls

The object balls are racked in a triangle shape, with the one ball at the top of the triangle and on the foot spot, the ten ball in the center of the triangle, and the other balls in arbitrary order as shown.

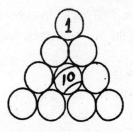

Diagram #7

EIGHT BALL

1. Summary

Eight Ball is played with fifteen object balls numbered one through fifteen and a cue ball. The object of the game is to pocket either the solid-colored group of balls, numbered one to seven, or the striped balls, numbered nine to fifteen, and after clearing your group of balls, to pocket the eight ball in a designated pocket. Once this is done, that player wins the game.

2.Beginning Play

2.1 ORDER OF PLAY

Order of play for the first game is determined by lag. The winner of the lag breaks the first rack. In subsequent games of the match, the winner of the previous game will break.

2.2 RACKING THE BALLS

The fifteen object balls are racked in a triangle shape, with the eight ball in the center and the other balls in arbitrary order as shown. The object ball at the top of the diamond should be centered on the foot spot.

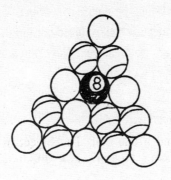

Diagran #6

2.3 Break Shot

The player to break has the cue ball in hand behind the head string. The rules governing the break shot are the same as for other shots except:

(a) Soft breaking is not allowed and is a foul. The breaker must attempt an "open," or hard, break. A referee, if present, may rule that a player did not attempt to break hard and may call a warning or a foul. The referee is not obligated to give a warning. If he calls a foul, the balls will be re-racked and the opponent will be awarded the break and ball in hand after the break.

(b) An attempt to break that results in the cue ball crossing the head string, but not hitting the rack, is a foul.

(c) If a referee is present and judges that the shooter is deliberately "passing" his obligation to break the rack, the opponent gets the break and ball in hand after the break.

(d) If the cue ball is pocketed or driven off the table, the incoming player has cue ball in hand behind the head string. All object balls that are pocketed will stay down, and the incoming player has choice or "open table."

(e) If a player pockets the eight ball during a legal break, he wins the game. If the player commits a foul during the break and the eight ball is pocketed, he loses the game.

3. After the Break

Here are some examples of situations that can arise immediately following the break shot:

(a) A single ball is pocketed. If, for example, it were the six ball, the breaker's group of balls would be the "solids," or low-numbered, object balls. From this point on, he must strike the solids first and pocket a solid to continue his inning.

(b) If one of each group of balls is pocketed—for example, the three ball and ten ball—the table would be open and the breaker has his choice of which group of balls he would like to shoot at on his second shot. Since it is open table, he may shoot a combination involving a stripe and a solid. The ball that is pocketed after the combination would be his group of balls from then on. If he were to miss on his second shot, his opponent would have open table.

(c) If two of one group of balls and one of the other group are pocketed—for example, the twelve, fourteen, and five balls—the table is open. The breaker has his choice of which group of balls he would like to shoot at on his second shot.

(d) If there are no object balls pocketed, the incoming player has the same options of open table as in (b) above.

4. Continuing Play

A player continues to shoot until he misses, fouls, or wins the game. If the player misses or fouls, the other player begins his inning and shoots until he misses, fouls, or wins.

4.1 COMBINATION SHOTS

To play a legal combination shot, the shooter must strike his type ball first and pocket his type ball. A player may use his opponent's ball in a combination only if he strikes his type ball first and pockets it. (Example: Player's type ball is solid. He then shoots the three ball into the twelve ball into the six ball and pockets the six ball.) You may strike the eight ball first during a combination.

4.2 SHOOTING THE WRONG TYPE OF BALL

Occasionally it occurs after the break, or at any time during the game, for that matter, that a player mistakenly starts shooting the wrong category of balls. Although it is sportsmanlike for the sitting player to remind the shooting player that he is about to

foul by shooting the wrong category of balls, it is not a requirement for the sitter to do so. Once the shooter has hit the wrong
category of balls, the foul has occurred whether the ball is
pocketed or not. If the ball is pocketed, it is permissible, though
not recommended, that the sitting player allow the shooting
player to continue shooting his balls in until he feels inclined to
call the foul.

The shooting player can escape penalty by quietly realiz-
ing his error and returning to shoot the correct category of balls
and legally contacting one of them before his opponent calls
foul, or by finishing off the wrong category of balls and legally
contacting the eight ball prior to his opponent's calling a foul. In
other words, the sitting player must call the foul before the
shooter returns to the correct category and legally contacts one
ball or before the shooter pockets the remaining balls of the
wrong category and legally contacts the eight ball. Before any
foul has occurred, the shooter may also avoid penalty by asking
the sitting player which category of balls he has. The sitting
player must tell him the truth. If a referee is present, he is
obligated to call the foul as soon as he is aware of it, but the
shooter may still avoid penalty (as above) if the referee fails to
call the foul.

4.3 BALL TO A RAIL

After the shooter contacts his type ball first, any object ball or
the cue ball must be driven to a rail or the shot is a foul and the
incoming player has ball in hand.

4.4 SAFETIES

A player may shoot a safety shot instead of attempting to pocket an object ball. This is usually done when it is not likely or possible to pocket an object ball. A player does not have to call a safety. A player's turn at the table ends after he has executed an attempted safety, unless he legally pockets a ball of his category—in which case he must continue shooting.

5. Standard Fouls

When a player commits a standard foul (see "Standard Fouls" under the General Rules section), he must relinquish his turn at the table. All balls pocketed on the foul will stay down. The incoming player is awarded ball in hand; prior to his first shot, he may place the cue ball anywhere on the table. If a player fouls during the other player's inning, the shooter is awarded ball in hand. If the foul had an effect on the position of the balls, the referee will restore the position if requested to do so by the shooter. If a player commits several standard fouls on one shot, they are counted as only one foul.

5.1 BAD HIT
If the first object ball contacted by the cue ball is not the player's type of ball, it is a foul. The incoming player is awarded cue ball in hand.

5.2 SPLIT HIT
If a player whose group of balls are the stripes contacts a striped object ball and a solid object ball at the same time, and the referee calls a split hit, it is a foul. He must contact only *his* group of balls first.

6. How to Win

A player wins the game when he has legally pocketed his type balls first and then legally pockets the eight ball in a designated pocket.

6.1 CALL THE EIGHT

A player only has to call the pocket that he will attempt to make the eight ball in. It does not matter how that ball reaches the pocket. When playing the last of your type ball, you cannot pocket the eight ball at the same time.

7. Loss of Game

It is loss of game if:

(a) The opponent legally pockets all of his type balls and the eight ball.

(b) The shooter alters the course of (or fouls while it is moving) a rolling eight ball or alters the course of (or fouls while it is moving) the cue ball when shooting at the eight ball.

(c) A player causes the eight ball to leave the playing surface (i.e., it ends up on the floor).

(d) A player pockets the eight ball but does not designate the pocket it went in before the shot.

(e) A player pockets the eight ball before his type of balls are cleared from the table.

(f) A player pockets the eight ball in a pocket other than the one designated.

(g) A player fouls when pocketing the eight ball.

Note: Missing the eight ball with the cue ball gives your opponent ball in hand but is not "loss of game."

(h) When shooting the eight ball, the shooter pockets (scratches) the cue ball or knocks the cue ball off the table. It is "loss of game" whether the eight ball is pocketed or not.

Note: Where it is stated that a referee should decide a ruling, and there is not a referee or third person available, the players competing will decide the ruling.

ROTATION

1. Summary

Rotation is played with fifteen object balls, numbered one to fifteen, and a cue ball. On each shot, the first ball the cue ball contacts must be the lowest-numbered ball on the table, but the balls do not need to be pocketed in order. Players do not need to call any shot. If a player pockets any ball on a legal shot, he remains at the table for another shot, and continues until he misses, fouls, or wins the game. Points are determined by the face value of the object balls. The total number of possible points with all fifteen object balls is 120. To win the game, a player only needs to acquire 61 of those points.

2. Beginning Play

2.1 ORDER OF PLAY

The order of play is determined by lag. The winner of the lag may break the first rack or assign the break to his opponent. In subsequent games of the match, the winner of the previous game will have the option to break.

2.2 RACKING THE BALLS

The object balls are racked in a triangle shape with the one ball at the top of the diamond and on the foot spot, the two ball and three ball on the lower corners of the rack, and the fifteen ball in the center as shown. If the one ball is not touching both of the adjacent balls, the breaker may ask the referee to re-rack the balls prior to the break. The cue ball begins in hand behind the head string.

2.3 BREAK SHOT
The rules governing the break shot are the same as for other shots except that:

(a) If the cue ball is pocketed or driven off the table, the incoming player has cue ball in hand anywhere on the table, and all balls pocketed are spotted.

(b) The breaker must attempt an "open break": He must attempt to pocket a ball. Failure to do so is a standard foul.

(c) If the shooter attempts an open break and the cue ball crosses the head string but fails to contact the one ball first, this is considered a foul. The balls are re-racked and the incoming player has the option to break.

(d) On the shot immediately following a legal break, the shooter may play a push out (see "Push Out" in the General Rules section).

3. Continuing Play

3.1 AFTER THE BREAK
If the breaker pockets one or more object balls on a legal break, he continues to shoot until he misses, fouls, or wins the game. If

the player misses or fouls, the other player begins his inning and shoots until he misses, fouls, or wins.

3.2 BALL TO A RAIL

After contacting the lowest-numbered ball on the table first, any object ball or the cue ball must be driven to a rail or the shot is foul and the incoming player has cue ball in hand anywhere on the table.

3.3 SAFETIES

A player may shoot a safety shot instead of attempting to pocket an object ball. This is usually done when it is not likely or possible to pocket an object ball. A player does not have to call a safety. A player's turn at the table ends after he has executed an attempted safety.

3.4 WINNING

As stated earlier, a player must acquire 61 of the 120 possible points scored. It is possible that after the last ball is pocketed, the players' score is tied 60 to 60. In this case, the player who pockets the last ball is awarded one point and wins the game.

4. Standard Fouls

When a player commits a standard foul (see ''Standard Foul'' in the General Rules section), he must relinquish his turn at the table. All balls pocketed on an illegal shot will be spotted on the foot spot and the incoming player is awarded ball in hand.

4.1 BAD HIT

If the first object ball contacted by the cue ball is not the lowest-numbered ball on the table, the shot is foul.

4.2 SPLIT HIT

If the cue ball strikes two object balls at the same instant, and the referee calls a split hit, it is a foul. The lowest-numbered ball on the table must be the only object ball to be contacted first.

4.3 JUMPED OBJECT BALLS

Any time an object ball leaves the playing surface (other than being legally pocketed), it is a foul. The jumped object ball is spotted and the incoming player has cue ball in hand anywhere on the table.

Note: Where it is stated that a referee should decide a ruling, and there is not a referee or third person available, the players competing will decide the ruling.

Player Profiles

The next pages are dedicated to the outstanding players of the Professional Billiards Tour. Because of space, we were not able to list all of the titles earned by each player.

Players of the PBTA may be available for exhibitions, seminars, etc. For more information, please contact the

PBTA
P.O. Box 5599
Spring Hill, FL 34608
904-688-5837
fax 904-686-5515

JOHNNY ARCHER

Johnny Archer was born in Waycross, Georgia., in the year 1968. He began playing when he was eleven years old after becoming bored with video games. His parents bought him a pool table and, at age thirteen, he began playing in local tournaments. Johnny entered his first professional tournament at age seventeen and finished "in the money," besting top players along the way. He captured his first major title in 1991: the Sands Regent Championship in Reno, Nevada. Since then, he has been on a roll, including winning the World Nine Ball Championship and reaching the number-one spot on the Professional Tour's Point Standing. Johnny is a member of World Team Billiards. Minutes before the finals of a pool tournament, you might find Johnny "warming up" by playing a round of golf. He also enjoys playing basketball and tennis.

TITLES

1988	Huebler Cup Champion	Ft. Collins, Co.
1990	Tara Open Champion	Atlanta, Ga.
1991	Spring Fling Champion	Raleigh, N.C.
1991	Sands Regent XIII Champion	Reno, Nev.
1991	Last Call for 9 Ball Champion	Las Vegas, Nev.
1992	Cleveland All-Around Champion	Cleveland, Oh.
1992	World 9 Ball Champion	Taipei, Taiwan
1992	Sands Regency XV	Reno, Nev.

SPONSORS AND ENDORSEMENTS
AAA Billiards & North Coast Amusement for Schon Cues

JEFF CARTER

Jeff Carter was born in Janesville, Wisconsin, in 1951. When Jeff was fourteen years old, he went into his first pool room. Someone he knew was playing and Jeff asked if he could hit a ball. Jeff became instantly mesmerized. His first professional event was in 1978 in St. Louis, Missouri. He is six-time Wisconsin State Champion and most recently won the Lexington One Pocket Championship. Jeff is the house professional at Muddlars Pool Hall in Chicago. He enjoys the outdoors, hiking, exercising and birdwatching.

TITLES
1978-87	Wisconsin State 14.1 & 9 Ball Champion
1980	Port Angles 9 Ball Champion
1984, '85	Midwest Open Champion
1984	Red's One Pocket Runner-Up
1988	Joey Spaeth Memorial Runner-Up
1989	Knoxville 9 Ball Open Runner-Up

| 1990 | World Champion 9 Ball Runner-Up |
| 1990 | Lexington One Pocket Champion |

OTHER ACCOMPLISHMENTS AND CREDITS
Television appearance on "Eurosport"
Feature writer for *Billiards Digest*

SPONSORS AND ENDORSEMENTS
Endorses Pechauer Cues from Greenbay, Wis.

KIM DAVENPORT

Kim Davenport was born in 1955 in a town called McAlester, in Oklahoma. When he was ten years old, he walked into his first pool room. At that time, his friends could not understand why he began to spend all his time playing pool. Now that Kim is a champion of the sport, he says his friends understand why he was so devoted to the sport. Kim won his first professional event in 1985, the Bowling Green Open, and in 1990 was named "Player of the Year" by *Billiards Digest*. He is co-owner of Championship Billiards in Modesto, California. Kim's other interests include golf, hunting, and gardening.

TITLES

1985	Bowling Green Open Champion
1987	Tarheel Classic Champion
1988	Eastern States 9 Ball Champion
1988	Japan Cup Champion
1989	U.S. Open (Runner-Up)

1989	Lexington All-Star Open Champion
1989	Greensboro Open Champion
1989	McDermott Masters Champion
1990	Brunswick Challenge Cup Champion
1990	Memorial Day Open Champion
1990	B.C. Open Champion
1990	Sands Regent XII Champion
1990	World Open 9 Ball (fourth place)
1992	Lexington All-Star Open Champion
1992	Bicycle Club Invitational (runner-up)

OTHER ACCOMPLISHMENTS AND CREDITS

| 1990 | *Billiards Digest* "Player of the Year" |
| 1990 | *Pool & Billiards* "Co-Player of the Year" |

SPONSORS AND ENDORSEMENTS
Endorses Tru-Tip Shaper

ERNESTO DOMINQUEZ

Ernesto Dominguez was born in Chihuahua, Mexico, in 1955. At thirteen, he found employment at a nearby billiards parlor. Ernesto's playing career began immediately, and he was competing daily. In 1974, although he moved to the United States, he did not play in his first professional event until 1982. This event was the Miller Lite tournament held at Caesar's Palace in Las Vegas, in which thousands of players qualified. Ernesto placed second. His talents have also enabled him to place in tournaments all over the world, including those in countries like Germany, Sweden, and Japan. Besides playing pool, Ernesto enjoys all types of sports.

TITLES

1982	Caesar's Palace Miller Lite 8 Ball (Runner-Up)
1983	Caesar's Palace Lake Tahoe (fifth place)
1986	Phoenix 8 Ball Open Champion

1988	Imperial Palace 8 Ball Champion
1989	Osaka Japan 9 Ball (Runner-Up)
1990	Tokyo Japan 9 Ball (Runner-Up)
1990	Vajo Sweden 9 Ball (third place)
1991	Sands Regent (third place)
1991	Munich Germany 9 Ball (fifth place)
1992	Manila Philippines 9 Ball (fifth place)
1992	Tokyo Japan 9 Ball (fifth place)

OTHER ACCOMPLISHMENTS AND CREDITS
Member of World Team Billiards, Mexican Team Television Appearances on major Los Angeles networks

ROGER GRIFFIS

Roger Griffis was born in Austin, Texas, in 1956. When he was a child, Roger played pool occasionally and dreamed of competing with Willie Mosconi and "Minnesota Fats." It wasn't until he was fourteen years old that the game became more serious to him. A Billiards parlor opened in Austin. Roger and his friends went there to watch the "big-time" players. When an old man with a big mustache threw a rack of balls on the table and pocketed them all without missing, Roger knew this was the place for him to learn the game. It wasn't until 1989 that he played in his first professional event, the Sands Regent in Reno, Nevada. In addition to playing pool, he enjoys cards and golfing.

TITLES

1990	Hollywood Open 9 Ball Champion
1990	Arizona 8 Ball Champion
1990	Spring Classic 9 Ball Champion

| 1990 | Sands Regency (Runner-Up) |
| 1992 | Pro Tour Championship |

SPONSORS AND ENDORSEMENTS
Pool & Billiards magazine

CECIL "BUDDY" HALL

Cecil "Buddy" Hall was born in Metropolis, Illinois, in the year 1945. He began playing pool at age fourteen, instantly loved the game, and has been playing ever since. He is nicknamed "The Rifleman," and has won over seventy titles during his career. He won his first professional title in 1974 at the Dayton Open in Ohio, and continues to win major titles to this day. Buddy is known by his peers as having one of the smoothest pool-shooting strokes on the tour. With more than thirty years devoted to the game, he has earned much respect for his playing ability as well as for his personality. Buddy has a new book that will be on the market soon: *Rags to Rifleman, Then What?* His other interests include fishing, baseball, football, and basketball.

TITLES
1974-84	Five Times Dayton Ohio Champion
1974, '76, '78	Citris Open Champion

1982, '84	Lake Tahoe Champion
1989	Memphis Open Champion
1989	Moline Open Champion
1991	Int'l 9 Ball Classic Champion
1991	Capitol City Open Champion
1991	Greensboro [N.C.] Open Champion
1991	U.S. Open Champion
1992	Rack M Up Classic Champion
1992	Winner Challenge of Champions
1992	Sands Regency XV Champion (Runner-Up)

OTHER ACCOMPLISHMENTS AND CREDITS

1982, '91 "Player of the Year"

Televised appearances on ESPN

SPONSORS AND ENDORSEMENTS

Lenoard Bludworth-Buddy Hall signature line of cues

Sure Shot Tip Shaper-Dead Nickle

Sure Shot Slick Stick

ALLEN HOPKINS

Allen Hopkins, nicknamed "Young Hoppy," was born in 1951 in Cranford, New Jersey. He entered the pocket billiards world by playing "checker pool" at age seven. Around that time, he picked up his first pool cue and ran ten consecutive balls on a six-foot table. Allen entered his first tournament when he was twelve years old against men at least twice his age—and won. His high run at thirteen years of age was an astonishing 110 consecutive balls. He played his first professional event when he was seventeen, the U.S. Open 14.1 Championships, and finished fifth. Since then, Allen has amazed the pool world with his talents, earning championships in all games: Nine Ball, Ten Ball, Straight Pool, and One Pocket. These championships include six World titles. In straight pool, he has a current high run of 410 consecutive balls. As current president of the MPBA, Allen devotes much of his time to the long-range goals of the pro tour. He also enjoys golfing as a pastime.

TITLES

1973	U.S. Tournament of Champions
1974, '75, '76, '89	New Jersey State 9 Ball Champion
1977	PPPA World 14.1 Champion
1977, '82	U.S. Open 9 Ball Champion
1979	Baltimore Bullet World 9 Ball Champion
1979, '80, '81	World 9 Ball Invitational Champion
1984	Texas River City Open 9 Ball Champion
1984	Meucci World 9 Ball Champion
1986, '87	Japan World Open Champion
1987	Eastern States 9 Ball Champion
1989	Coors Valley Forge Classic Champion
1990	Cleveland 10 Ball Champion
1990	Rocket City Invitational Champion
1991	World One Pocket Champion
1991	Rak M Up Champion

OTHER ACCOMPLISHMENTS AND CREDITS

Current president, Men's Professional Billiards Association
Television appearances on ABC, CBS, NBC, ESPN, USA, PRIME Commentator for ESPN and Co-Commentator for CBS Sports

SPONSORS AND ENDORSEMENTS

Diamond Professional Products Company
Barco Products

DAVID HOWARD

David Howard, nicknamed "Little David," was born in Jacksonville, Florida, in 1953. When David was nine years old, he would help his best friend spend his $20-a-week allowance on movies, bowling, and shooting pool. David soon noticed his natural talent and pursued the sport. He began winning tournaments at the age of twelve. In 1978, his first professional tournament was the Southern Open in Baton Rouge, Louisiana—which he won. David is the owner of Little David's Pocket Billiards in Jacksonville. He is currently a member of World Team Billiards. He enjoys water sports such as jet skiing, boating, and fishing. Golfing is another of David's favorite pastimes.

TITLES
1978   Southern Open Champion
1979, '83   U.S. Open 9 Ball (Runner-Up)

1982	Mike Massey Open Champion
1982, '86	U.S. Open 9 Ball Champion
1983	World 9 Ball (Runner-Up)
1984, '85	Spring Open Champion
1986	Sands Regent (Runner-Up)
1986	Atlanta Open Champion
1988	Joey Spaeth Memorial Champion
1988	Asian World Cup Champion
1988	Southern California Invitational Champion
1988	Hard Times Open Champion
1990	Cleveland 10 Ball Classic (Runner-Up)
1991	Dufferin 9 Ball Classic Champion

OTHER ACCOMPLISHMENTS AND CREDITS

Appearances in *P.M.* magazine, and on ESPN, "Chalk It Up," "Trick Shots," and in commercials for Meucci Originals and Aspen Colorado Billiards.

SPONSORS AND ENDORSEMENTS

Meucci Originals professional staff member with a private cue line.

Sponsored by Dynamo Home Products, Ft. Worth, Tex.

MIKE LEBRON

Mike Lebron was born in 1934 in Yabucoa, Puerto Rico. When he was entering his teens, he would walk past a Billiards parlor every day on his way to school. Hearing the click of the pool balls was an inviting sound for Mike, and when the owner offered him a small job there he accepted happily. This was where his career in pocket billiards began.

He is now a permanent resident of the United States. With continuous achievements, such as winning the 1991 Challenge of Champions in Las Vegas, Nevada, Mike has become a fierce competitor on the professional tour. Besides his love for pocket billiards, Mike also enjoys many other sports.

TITLES
1985   U.S. Open (Runner-Up)
1985, '86   B.C. Open (Runner-Up)

1988	Governor's Cup (Runner-Up)
1988	Miller Time Open (Runner-Up)
1988	U.S. Open Champion
1988	Pool Hall Classic Champion
1990	Glass City Open Champion
1990	Taipei [Taiwan] Open Champion
1991	Munich Masters (Runner-Up)
1991	Int'l 9 Ball Classic (Runner-Up)
1991	Challenge of Champions Champion

JIMMY MATAYA

Jimmy Mataya, also known as ''Pretty Boy Floyd,'' was born in 1949 in Lansing, Michigan. As a young boy, he would go to the local gym, which was equipped with a pool table. Since it was during the time of the movie *The Hustler*, pool seemed like the thing to do. He tried it, learned to play very well, and at the same time met a lot of nice and interesting people along the way. Since 1965, Jimmy has supported the national professional organization by consistently playing in the events. He has won several major titles as well as numerous state titles during his career. His athletic ability is prominent in all types of sports activities.

TITLES
1967   Motor City Open Champion
1971   World 9 Ball Champion

1972	Stardust World All-Around Champion
1976	All-Around Champion
1977	World 8 Ball Champion
1978	Port Angeles Open Champion
1986	Pepsi Open Champion
1988	World Pro-Am Champion
1991	McDermott Masters Runner-Up

OTHER ACCOMPLISHMENTS AND CREDITS
1988 Inducted into the Michigan Pocket Billiards Hall of Fame
1989 Inducted into the Greater Lansing Sports Hall of Fame
1992 Commentator for "World Team Billiards" on Prime Network

SPONSORS AND ENDORSEMENTS
Endorses "Billiards Instruction for the Mind" tapes
True Q Tip Shapers & Cue Burnishers

STEVE MIZERAK

Steve Mizerak, nicknamed "The Miz," was born in 1944. Steve got his start in pool at the age of four through the help of his father, who was New Jersey State Champion for many years. Steve began playing pool professionally when he was thirteen years old. Since that time, numerous titles have been added to his collection of victories, dating back as far as 1966, the Indiana State Championship. He has a current high run in straight pool of 384 consecutive balls and was inducted into the Hall of Fame in 1980. In 1979, Steve's appearance on the Miller Lite Beer commercial attracted a large amount of media attention for pocket billiards. Steve has published five teaching books and three videotapes. He presently holds the coveted title of 1982, '83 and '84 World Pocket Billiards Champion. As do many other players, Steve enjoys golfing as a pastime.

TITLES

1970, '71, '72, '73	U.S. Open Champion
1982, '83	World Champion
1967-77	Eight Time New Jersey State Champion
1971, '73, '74, '75	U.S. Masters Champion
1973	Eastern States Classic Champion
1977	New York State 14.1 Champion
1980	Eastern State 9 Ball Champion
1988	U.S. Open 14.1 Champion
1991	Hard Times Open Champion
1992	Rak M Up Classic (Runner-Up)
1992	Legends of One Pocket (Runner-Up)

OTHER ACCOMPLISHMENTS AND CREDITS

Maker of Steve Mizerak Custom Cues

1983 "Man of the Year" Award

Television appearances on ABC, CBS, NBC, ESPN, "David Letterman," "That's Incredible," "Merv Griffin," and magazine articles in *Time*, *Playboy*, *People*, and *Harness Race*

JOSE PARICA, JR.

Jose Parica, Jr., was born in the Philippines. His father owned a pool room and was also a very good player. Jose watched closely and learned very quickly when players would come to challenge his father. At age seventeen, Jose was considered possibly the best player in his country. His real recognition came when he placed fourth in a prestigious tournament held in Japan. His first title was also earned in Japan, when he defeated the number-one-ranked Japanese player.

Jose began competing in the United States in 1979. That year, at his first U.S. tournament, he tied for ninth place. After an absence of playing in the United States, Jose returned in 1986 and is now consistently competing on the pro tour. He is also an amateur Jai Alai player, and in earlier years was a Golden Glove champion in boxing.

TITLES

1979	Philippic Open 8 Ball Champion
1980	International All-Around Champion
1986	World Open Clyde Childress
1986	World Classic Cup
1987, '88	International Open
1988	World Pro 9 Ball Champion
1988	Tokyo Open
1988	Japan Open
1991	Sands Last Call for 9 Ball
1992	Philippines 9 Ball Open

JAMES REMPE

"King" James Rempe was born in 1947 in Dixon City, Pennsylvania. Introduced into the game at age six, he turned professional at twenty-two. Jim's role in pocket billiards has taken him all over the world. During his travels he has earned titles in many different countries, including England, Sweden, New Zealand, and Japan—not to mention many in the United States. Jim is a member of World Team Billiards Team America. His television appearances have included "Challenge of Champions," "Good Fishing America," "Baltimore Bullet," and many more. Jim enjoys fine dining around the world. Another of his favorite pastimes is fishing.

\TITLES
1971, '72, '75	U.S. Masters 14.1
1972, '75	World 9 Ball
1975	U.S. Masters One Pocket
1976	Masters Invitational All-Around

1977	World Invitation 9 Ball, 14.1 and Grand Champion
1979	All Pro Japan 9 Ball
1980	PPPA Invitational World 9 Ball
1980	King of the Tables (Snooker-Pool)
1984	World One Pocket
1984	B & I Masters-english Pool Champ
1985	Yugo World Pool Challenge (vs. Steve Davis)
1986	Last Call for 9 Ball
1987	B.C. Open 9 Ball
1989	National 14.1
1992	Sands Regent XIII

OTHER ACCOMPLISHMENTS AND CREDITS

Inducted into the Pennsylvania Hall of Fame

Video credits: ''Pool School,'' ''Power Pool,'' ''Trick Shots''

Appearances on ABC, CBS, BBC, ESPN, USA, NIN TV

SPONSORS AND ENDORSEMENTS

Sponsors and endorses Meucci Original Custom Cues

Connelly Tables

Sportsmaster Table Covers

J.R. Trainer-Ball

J.R. Insoles Magnetic

EFREN REYES

Efren Reyes was born in the Philippines in 1954. He began playing pocket billiards when he was only eight years old. His natural ability and dedication to pocket billiards has enabled Efren to earn many titles around the world, including the National Championship for many years in the Philippines. He has been playing on the professional tour, and is acknowledged as one of today's best-all-around players. Efren's knowledge of the game is expansive. He has easily demonstrated his range of abilities through the wide variety among his titles. He recently added a victory in the Willards International Eight Ball Championships in 1992 -- his frist major eight ball event. When Efren is not amazing people with his pool-playing stroke, he is enjoying a game of chess.

TITLES
1983-91   National Champion, Philippines

1985	Red's 9 Ball Open Champion
1986	Sands Regent Champion (back to back)
1986	Rocky Mountain Open Champion
1988	McDermott Masters Champion
1989	Ocean Cup Champion,Osaka,Japan
1990	International 9 Ball Champion, Osaka
1991	Taipei [Taiwan] World Cup Champion
1992	Tokyo World Open 9 Ball Champion
1992	Willards International 8 Ball Champion

SPONSORS AND ENDORSEMENTS

AMF-PUYAT Bowling and Billiards

MIKE SIGEL

Mike Sigel was born in Rochester, New York, in 1953. His parents bought a table for his older brother when Mike was thirteen. Mike has been playing ever since. He turned professional at age twenty and won his first major title in 1975: the U.S. Open Nine Ball Championship. Mike has captured that title five times in total, is a four-time World Straight Pool Champion, and, to date, is the youngest male member of the Hall of Fame. He was technical advisor of the popular movie *Color of Money*, and his credentials have enabled Mike to tape four videos on pocket Billiards instruction. He was voted by his peers one of the "Best All Around Players," and is a member of World Team Billiards. Mike enjoys his free time playing golf, traveling, and he has a great love for fishing.

TITLES

1975, '76, '80, '83, '86   US Open Champion

1976, '77	World 9 Ball Champion
1977	Masters All-Around Champion
1978	US Open One Pocket
1979	World Open Champion
1981	PPPA World Open Champion
1981	Caesar's Tahoe Classic
1982	Music City 9 Ball Champion
1983	Caesar's 9 Ball Champion
1985, '89	World 14.1 Champion
1985, '86	Glass City Open Champion
1985, '86, '88, '89	Sands Regent Open
1986	Resorts Int'l Champion
1988	Rack M Up Classic
1988, '89	Challenge Cup
1989	B.C. Open
1992	Bicycle Club Invitational

SPONSORS AND ENDORSEMENTS
Player adviser for Vitalie & Sterling Tables
Representative for Joss Professional Cues

OTHER CREDITS AND ACCOMPLISHMENTS
1981, '89   *Billiards Digest* "Player of the Year"
1983   *Billiards News* "Player of the Year"
1989   Inducted into the BCA Hall of Fame
1989   Technical Adviser to the movie *The Color of Money*
Appearances on ABC, CBS, ESPN
Creator of instructional tape "Mike Sigel's Winning Edge"

EARL STRICKLAND

Earl Strickland, known as "Earl the Pearl," was born in Roseboro, North Carolina, in 1961. He began playing pool at the age of nine and entered his first tournament when he was fifteen—in which he finished third. He turned professional at the early age of twenty, and since then Earl's impressive career includes four World Championships and being five times named "Player of the Year." He is currently a member of World Team Billiards. In just one decade, Earl has earned numerous titles. He is also an avid golf and tennis player.

TITLES

1982	Dayton Open Champion
1982, '87, '88, '89,'92	Akron Open Champion
1983	Lake Tahoe Classic Champion
1984, '91, '92	McDermott Masters Champion

1984, '87	U.S. Open 9 Ball Champion
1984	Caesar's Palace 9 Ball Champion
1985	Clyde Childress Memorial Champion
1985, '87	Charlotte Open Champion
1988	Caesar's Palace Brunswick World Open Champ
1988, '90	Lexington All-Star Open Champion
1988	Augusta 9 Ball Open
1990	World 9 Ball Champion
1990, '92	Sands Regency Champion
1991	WPA World Championships
1992	Los Angeles Open Champion

OTHER ACCOMPLISHMENTS AND CREDITS

Television appearances on ESPN, Home Team Sports Network, Toledo Ohio News, Los Angeles News, sports and news networks in Asia and Europe, and various other news networks in the United States, as well as "Good Evening."

SPONSORS AND ENDORSEMENTS
Sponsored by Cuetec Cue Company, Taichung, Taiwan
Endorses Steel Stix Cue Company
Endorses D&R Championship Billiards Fabrics, Chicago
Endorses Diamond Professional Tables, Clemmons, N.C.

NICK VARNER

Nick Varner was borne in Owensboro, Kentucky, in 1948. He began playing pool at the age of five, when his father bought a pool room in Grandview, Indiana. In those days, it was common to see Nick on a Coke case getting basic tips from his father. Nick attended Purdue University. During his freshman year, he located a table on campus and for the next three years he practiced nearly every day, eventually winning two ACU-I National Championships. Since then, Nick has added many titles and accomplishments to his career, including being voted one of the three best-all-around players by his peers. Nick is an owner of Breakers Billiards in Owensboro, Kentucky, and is the newest member of the Hall of Fame. He also enjoys golf, gardening, and tennis.

TITLES

1969, '70   ACU-I National Champion

1980, '86	World Open 14.1 (PPPA)
1980	BCA National 8-Ball Champion
1982	World 9 Ball Champion (PPPA)
1983, '87	McDermott Masters
1985	Zurich Open 9 Ball
1988, '89	Sands Regent 9 Ball Open
1988	Glass City Open 9 Ball
1989, '91	Rak M Up Classic
1989	Governor's Cup 9 Ball
1989	Glass City Open 9 Ball
1989	Brunswick World Open 9 Ball
1989	Lexington All-Star Open
1989, '90	U.S. Open 9 Ball
1990	World Series Challenge

OTHER ACCOMPLISHMENTS AND CREDITS

1980, '89	*Billiards Digest* ''Player of the Year''
1991	MPBA ''Sportsperson of the Year''
1992	Inducted into the BCA Hall of Fame

Author of *Winning Pool & Trick Shots*

Appearances on ABC, CBS, ESPN, USA, Tempo

SPONSORS AND ENDORSEMENTS

Player Representative for Peter Vitalie Pool Table Company and Sterling Pool Table Company

Player Representative for Falcon Cues

Endorses 'Nick Varner Tip Tool' by George Endorses Sports Advantage Products

Endorses Q-Clean

DALLAS WEST

Dallas West was born in 1941. He walked by a billiards parlor on the way to school one day, and was so small he could hardly see inside. The sound of pool balls clicking raised his curiosity. For a time, Dallas was not allowed in, since the legal age to enter a billiards parlor was sixteen and Dallas was only twelve at the time. But his persistence won and the owner made an acception. When he was twenty years old, he entered his first big local event, a city championship, and finished second. The next year, Dallas came back to win that event. Dallas has played in over twenty "World" tournaments since that time, and has titles in Nine Ball, Straight Pool, and Three Cushion. He is still competing on the pro tour and has a current high run in straight pool of 420. He is the owner of Dallas West Billiards in Rockford, Illinois. Besides playing pool, he loves golf and fishing.

TITLES

1965-75	Six Times Midwest Open 14.1 Champion
1965-75	Three Times Motor City Open 14.1 Champion
1965-75	Ten Times Illinois State 14.1 Champion
1965-75	Ten Times Illinois State 9 Ball Champion
1965-75	Six Times Midwest Open 9 Ball Champion
1975	U.S. Open 14.1 Champion
1977	Midwest Open 3 Cushion Champion
1978	Chicago Classic 3 Cushion Champion
1978	Drexel Open 3 Cushion Champion
1978	Autumn Open 14.1 Champion
1979	World Open 9 Ball Champion
1983	U.S. Open 14.1 Champion
1992	U.S. Open 14.1 (Runner-Up)

SPONSORS AND ENDORSEMENTS
Omega Cues (co-sponsor)

CARSON J. WILEY

Carson J. Wiley, nicknamed "C.J.," was born in Green City, Missouri, in 1964. There was not much to do for a boy seven years old in a town whose population was only 627. For this reason, C.J. took up playing pocket billiards. By the time he was eleven, he was running racks of Eight Ball and was the toughest competition in town. Although C.J. is new on the pro tour, he has made an impressive entrance, finishing his first year in the tour point rankings top sixteen at the end of 1991. C.J. is the co-owner of Champs Billiards in Dallas, Texas. He also enjoys play ing golf and tennis, and is exceptional at the art of Chung Moo Doe.

TITLES

| 1982 | National High School Champion |
| 1986 | World Series of Tavern Pool Champion |

1991	Dufferin Classic (fourth place)
1991	Sands Regent (fifth place)
1992	L.A. Open (third place)

AUTOGRAPHS

Billiards Etiquette

1. Stay seated while your opponent is at the table. If there are not any seats available, stand quietly at least four feet away from the table.

2. Let your opponent shoot all necessary balls, but do not concede any balls. In professional tournaments, a player is fined if he or she concedes any balls.

3. Wait until you approach the table to chalk your cue stick. If you use the chalk when leaving the table, your opponent may need it.

4. Please do not use any loud, abusive, or profane language. Our sport's reputation is at stake when you do this.

5. During competition it is not sportsmanlike to carry on a conversation with anyone while your opponent is at the table.

6. Wait until your opponent has completed his inning before you begin to approach the table.

7. It is a forfeit of match if you break apart your cue stick before the match is over. If you have to change shafts, notify your opponent before doing so.

8. Be aware of players on the tables surrounding yours. Try not to bump into them while they are shooting.

9. If you need to borrow a bridge or rack from the table next to you, quietly wait until the players there are done shooting before approaching them.

10. Do not sit on any pool table. This may take it out of level!

11. Keep any drinks, food, or cigarettes away from the pool table.

12. When you are finished using a pool table, wait until the balls are brought up to the counter before notifying the counter person to take you off the clock. Yelling this across the room will disrupt other players.

13. If you are in the direct line of a person's shot, stay as still as possible until he or she has finished shooting.

What Does It Take
to Become a Champion?

Champions are often asked this question: "What does it take to become a champion?" We have polled some of today's top pocket billiards champions and this is what they had to say.

ALLEN HOPKINS
"To become a champion, you must practice often and seriously. If you don't take your practice time seriously, it's not going to help you when you get into competition and you need to perform. The most important thing about being a champion is consistency and knowledge. The champions are also the ones who perform under pressure. When they have to make a ball or they have to execute position shots or safety shots, the ones who do that more consistently at the time when they need it is what makes them win tournaments."

BUDDY HALL
"The difference between a shortstop and a champion would be that the champion actually has the ability to improve while he is playing an opponent. He doesn't have to go home and practice what he sees, I mean, he adapts it to his game as soon as he sees it."

EARL STRICKLAND

"It takes a lot of hard work and dedication to be good at anything. Some people, like myself, are born with a God-given talent, and you just have to pursue it. But for most people, it takes a lot of hard work and dedication. You have to live a clean life, stay away from drugs and alcohol, have good hobbies. I think one of the reasons I became such a good player is because I really wanted it. I really loved the game, too. I think you really have to love your sport to be good at it."

NICK VARNER

"To become a champion, I think what's real important is that you concentrate hard on every ball. A lot of people think that to win tournaments they're thinking in terms of running racks or playing flawlessly, but I think what's really important is just trying as hard as you can on every shot to put the best stroke on it you can."

JIM REMPE

"The first thing you have to do is get the right basics. In other words, you should get lessons from a top player to make sure you are in the right stance at the table and have the right sighting. Then it's all the three D's. Dedication, determination, and desire. You need a love for the game, thats what it takes to do anything well. By love for the game, I mean desire."

JOHNNY ARCHER

"It takes a lot of hard work and dedication. I think you have to devote yourself, and if you have enough talent and you have enough fight to try and win, you can do it."

KIM DAVENPORT

"To become a champion, you have to practice and sacrifice a lot. I sacrificed a lot when I was young. Even though I worked hard at it, I was a natural and it seemed to come easier to me than others. The other important element to becoming a champion is that you must play against champions. If you are the best player at home, you must go somewhere and play the better players. That's the only way that I believe you can become a true top-notch champion."

Equipment Specifications

TABLE

Playing area   50" x 100" +/- 1/16"

Slate   Must be at least 1"thick and have wood or HDF backing.

Center of rail height   1 29/64" +/- 1/16"
K - 55 Profile

Location of diamonds in rail   3 11/16" from tip of rubber to center of diamond.

Height of table   30" +/- 1/2" from floor to bed of slate

Rail   Must be at least 5 1/2" wide including rubber

CLOTH

The PBTA recognizes Simonis 860 cloth as the official cloth of the tour.

LIGHTS

Suggested type: 4-8' fluorescent tubes, spaced evenly over 50 x 100" playing

surface using diffusing grid to
evenly disperse light and
eliminate shadows.

Distance   Should be located 80" from
                              floor.

Incandescent equivalent lighting is acceptable.

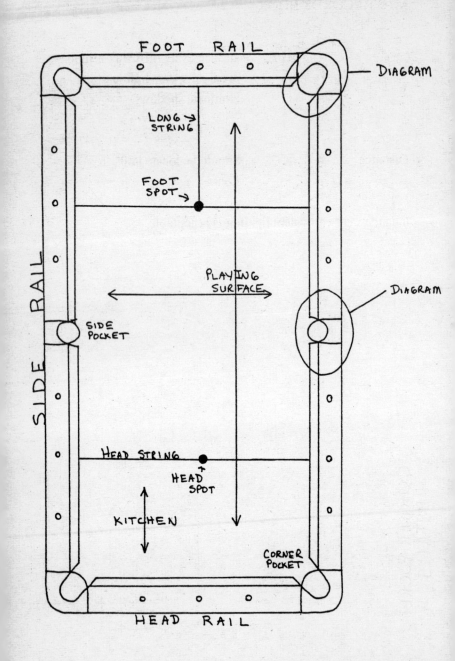

Diagram #1

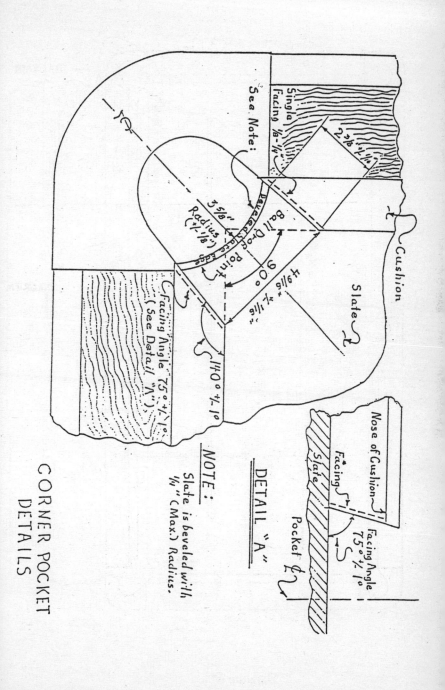

CORNER POCKET
DETAILS

Single
Facing ⅛"-¼"

See Note:

Cushion

2 ⅜"±⅛"

Developation

3 ⅝"
Radius
(±⅛")

Ball Drop
Point

Facing

90°

4 9/16"±1/16"

Slate

"Facing Angle" 75°±1°
(See Detail "A")

140°±1°

NOTE:
Slate is beveled with
⅛"(Max.) Radius.

DETAIL "A"

Nose of Cushion

Facing

Slate

Facing Angle
75°±1°

Pocket ℄

SIDE POCKET DETAILS

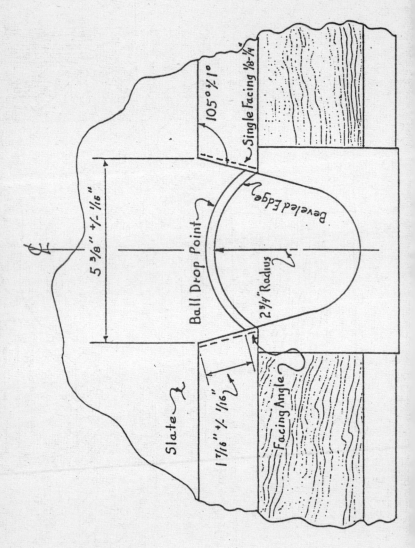

105° ±1°

Single Facing 1/8-1/4

Beveled Edge

Ball Drop Point

5 5/8" +/- 1/16"

2 3/4" Radius

Slate

1 7/16" +/- 1/16"

Facing Angle

Notes

JOIN THE PBTA NOW AND BECOME INVOLVED IN PROFESSIONAL POCKET BILLIARDS

Please check type of membership:

☐ Associate Member $25
☐ Semi-Pro $50
☐ Professional $100
☐ Touring Pro $100
☐ Network $100
☐ Patron $250

Send check or money order to:

PBTA

P.O. Box 5599

Spring Hill, FL 34608

(904) 688-5837

NAME _____

ADDRESS _____

CITY _____

STATE _____ ZIP _____

PHONE ( ) _____

PRO TOUR RULES FOR TELEVISION

1.   40 minute game clock.

2.   25 second shot clock. Player gets 25 seconds between shots which begins when all balls stop moving.

3.   Fouls on all balls.

4.   Trailing player breaks. When a match is tied, the player who was leading prior to the tied game gets the next break.

5.   Match is won by the player who wins the most games.

6.   If the match is tied after regulation time, then the players lag for the break and play one game to decide the winner of the match.

7.   If the 40 minute match shot clock expires during a game, the players must continue to play until that game is completed.

8.   Each player has two thirty second time outs per match. When a player wants to call time out, he must signal the referee who then will immediately call time out. The game clock and the shot clock will only be stopped by the official time keeper upon the referee's signal. If a player calls time out with no time outs available, he then must shoot the shot before his allotted time or it is a foul. At the end of the 30 second time out, the game clock and shot clock resume. If a player elects t execute a shot prior to the end of his 30

second time out, the game clock and shot clock will resume upon cue striking the cue ball.

9.   The game clock stops between racks. Then the referee signals the player and time keeper to start the game clock and the shot clock after he racks the balls. The player has 10 seconds to break the balls.

WORLD TEAM BILLIARDS
RULES/FORMAT

* **Five or six man teams.**

* **40 minutes of play divided into two, twenty-minute halves.**

* **Shot Clock:**
25 seconds to incoming player
20 seconds between shots

* **Pass or shoot option:**
Incoming player has the option to shoot or to pass the shot back to the opposing team (10 seconds to decide)

* **One (1) safety per game:**
Each team has the option to play 1 safety per game.
The opponent must shoot the shot after the safety is made.

* **Trailer breaks:**
The trailing team has the break until the leading team is tied at which time the team that gets tied will break.

* **Two time outs per half:**
Each team has a 30 second and a 60 second time out per half. No time outs in sudden death.

* **Sudden death (if tied at the end of 40 minutes):**
One game is played for the match.

* **Shot clock is activated when all balls stop moving**

* **Players turn (inning):**
Each team has a "line up", number 1 thru 6. Player must shoot in order. Player turn ends when he misses a shot or when he pockets the nine ball.

* **No push outs after the break.**

* **Finish games:**
If a game is underway when time expires in either half, the game must be completed.

CHALLENGE OF CHAMPIONS

Produced by Billiards International, LTD.

The 8 top ranked pro players compete for winner-take-all of $50,000 and the title "Champion of Champions."

RULES OF THE GAME

The game in all matches will be 9 Ball. After the break, the ball are pocketed in numerical order and the player who pockets the 9 ball wins the game. Quarterfinal matches will be race to 5 games (5 out of 9 games): semifinals and finals matches will be Two Sets, race to 5 games each set. In the event of tied sets, the players will lag for the break and decide the match with a 1 game tie-breaker.

1. The initial break will be decided by a lag. Thereafter the players will alternate on the break.

2. If 9 ball is made on the break, it will be spotted. Player at the table for the break continues shooting.

3. Pro rules will apply in the event of a cue ball scratch. During regular play, in the event of a cue ball scratch, all balls pocketed will stay down, excluding the 9 ball.

4. A foul will be called if player moves (or touches) either the cue ball or a number ball. Opposing player receives cue ball in hand.

5. Safeties will be allowed

6.   There will be a 30-second shot clock on each shot. If
      player fails to get off the shot, the referee will call a foul
      and opposing player receives cue ball in hand.

7.   A player cannot "luck" in the 9 ball and win a game. In
      such event, the 9 will be spotted and the game will
      continue. If player lucks n the 9 ball but does not make an
      object ball, the 9 is spotted and it becomes the
      opponents turn at the table.

8.   When shooting the 9 ball itself, player must make the ball
      in a designated pocket to win the game. Player must
      "call" the pocket before the shot. Combination and
      carom shots count as legitimate shots.

9.   During normal play, each player will be allowed one 30-
      second time out per match. the one time-out rule applies
      whether the match is race to 5 games, or two sets, race to
      5 games each set. The player must signal the referee and
      call "Time Out" before the normal 30-second limit
      between shots expires. The shot clock will then be reset
      to 30-seconds for the time our.

THE AUTHOR

Dawn Meurin began playing pool in earnest at age 23. Two years later, she became a touring pro on the Women's Professional circuit. Since then, her ranking on the tour have made her one of the top competitors in the sport. In 1988, she founded the "All About Pool" Magazine, covering copy also originated and organized five separate regional tours throughout the New England area. In 1993, she played an active role in producing the first "Super Billiards Expo", an International exposition featuring industry exhibitors as well as six professional and amateur tournaments. Her record as a Touring Pro as well as her deep commitment to the sport, resulted in her selection as editor of the "Official Billiards Rule Book." She currently resides in Pomona, New Jersey.

The PBTA and Dawn Meurin would like to thank the following for their contributions:

American Pool Players Association, Inc.
Johnny Archer
Matt Braun
Jeff Carter
Kim Davenport
Ernesto Domingues
Roger Griffis
Buddy Hall
Allen Hopkins
David Howard
Robert Jewett
Mike Lebron
Diane Mackey
Don Mackey
Francine Massey
Jimmy Mataya
Steve Mizerak
Jose Parica Jr.
James Rempe
Efren Reyes
Tony Seidl
Mike Shamos
Mike Sigel
Earl Strickland
Nick Varner
Dallas West
Carson J. Wiley

PRO BILLIARDS TOUR

Professional Billiards Tour Association Inc

PLAYER MEMBER AGREEMENT

This agreement made this _____ day of _____ 19 ____ by and between the

Men's Professional Billiards Association (hereinafter referred to as MPBA) and _____

_____ (hereinafter referred to as "Player Member").

Commencing on the date of this agreement and upon payment of the annual dues of $25.00, the applicant is granted "Player Member" membership in the MPBA.

The Player Member understands that they are bound to abide by the same code of conduct and ethics as the Semi-Professional, Professional, and Touring Professional members of this professional player association.

In addition, the Player Member is eligible to earn Pro Tour Qualifying Points in all events Recognized as a part of the Professional Billiards Tour Association's Regional Circuit.

Further, once a Player Member has accumulated 18 Qualifying Points (with at least 6 of the Qualifying Points earned in a Class AAA Regional Event), the Player Member is eligible to upgrade their membership status to Semi-Professional (upon written contract and payment of the required annual dues for this membership category) whereby they then become eligible to participate in Sanctioned Pro Tour events.

Player Members earn Qualifying Points by finishing in the top half of the field in Recognized Regional Tournaments in accordance with the following schedule:

1) Class A Event = 2 Points (Class A events have no Added Money requirement from the tournament organizer.)

2) Class AA Event = 3 Points (Class AA events require a "minimum" added to the purse of $1,000.)

3) Class AAA Event = 6 Points (Class AAA events require a "minimum" added to the purse of $3,000.)

Signed _____   Dated _____

(Please Print)

Name _____   SS # _____

Address _____   DL # _____

City/State/Zip _____   Date of Birth _____

Res. Ph. # _____   Wk. Ph. # _____

Mail this application with your $25 Annual Dues Payment to

Men's Professional Billiards Association
P.O. Box 5599
Spring Hill, Florida 34608

Professional Billiards Tour Association, Inc.

P.O. Box 5599   Spring Hill, Florida 34608   Phone (904) 688-5837 / Fax (904) 686-5515

REGIONAL CIRCUIT TOURNAMENT
"Recognition" Application

Date of Tournament _____ · Discipline (9-Ball, 8-Ball, etc.)_____
Title of Tournament _____ Table Size _____
Added Money _____
Entry Fee _____ Field Size _____
Format (single-double elimin., races to, etc.) _____

Tournament Site (name of billiard center or other facility) _____
Address (street, city, state, zip) _____
Individual/Firm Promoting Tournament_____ · _____
Telephones: (location)_____ (individual)_____

I, _____ (promoter), hereby request the RECOGNITION
by the Professional Billiards Tour Association, Inc. (PBTA), of the above listed tournament.

I certify that this event is in compliance with all local, state, and federal laws and regulations and that I will
hold the PBTA harmless against any and all claims or demands that may result from the production of this
event. I further understand that I assume all responsibility, financial and otherwise, for the staging and
producing of this event and that the PBTA assumes no financial responsibility, and that no implied PBTA
guarantee of prize funds or playing conditions is made.

I understand that the Men's Professional Billiards Association, along with the PBTA, reserve all rights to the
broadcast, rebroadcast, commercial video tape, or any other electronic media or photographic likeness
(excluding news coverage) connected with the competition of their professional players.

I understand that MPBA professional members who are eligible for the PBTA Pro Tour are also eligible to
enter all REGIONAL CIRCUIT tournaments.

I understand that MPBA "Player Members" (not eligible for the Pro Tour) can earn Pro Tour Qualifying Points
in this event by placing in the top 1/2 of the field. I further understand that it is my responsibility, as part of
this Recognition Agreement, to furnish the PBTA with a complete Roster of participants (including name,
address and telephone) along with the final place of finish of each contestant.

RECOGNITION FEE SCHEDULE:
■ When no money is added to the event: **$20.00** (Contact the PBTA for annual local event rate).
■ When $1,000.00 is added to event: **$50.00**.
■ When $3,000.00 is added to event: **$100.00**.
■ When the total added exceeds $5,000.00, the Recognition Fee will be **$25.00** for each $1,000.00 added.

Enclosed is the RECOGNITION FEE of $ _____ . I understand that the PBTA will
notify the billiard publications of this scheduled Regional Circuit Event and that this information will be made
available to all MPBA members in their next monthly Tour Newsletter, if the dates are applicable.

Signed_____ Dated_____

MAIL THIS APPLICATION ALONG WITH YOUR "RECOGNITION FEE" TO:
Professional Billiards Tour Association, P.O. Box 5599, Spring Hill, Florida 34608

PBTA Recognition Granted By: _____ (date) _____
POST APPROVED APPLICATION IN PROMINENT AREA DURING TOURNAMENT

(Applications and Fees must be received prior to the event for Recognition to be granted.)
For Further Information, Call: (904) 688-5837.